JUST WORDS

JUST WORDS

Understanding the Fullness of the Gospel

JACOB A. O. PREUS

CONCORDIA PUBLISHING HOUSE • SAINT LOUIS

To Sherry

Copyright © 2000 Concordia Publishing House
3558 S. Jefferson Avenue, St. Louis, MO 63118-3968
1-800-325-3040 • cph.org

Manufactured in the United States of America

Library of Congress Cataloging-in-Publication Data
Preus, Jacob A. O., 1953–
    Just words : understanding the fullness of the Gospel / Jacob A. O. Preus.
        p. cm.
Includes bibliographical references.
    ISBN 0-570-05378-1
    1. Salvation   2. Justification   I. Title.
    BT751.2 .P75 2000
    234—dc21   00-008496

2 3 4 5 6 7 8 9 10 11   26 25 24 23 22 21 20 19 18 17

Contents

Preface

In the preparation of this book, I owe a debt of gratitude to many people. To the men and women, both lay and clergy, who helped give shape to this project through their lively and thoughtful responses to my presentations (far and wide), I am thankful. To my many students, who through the years have kept me sharp and have genuinely informed the substance of this book, I owe thanks. To my colleagues at Concordia Seminary, who with ruthless kindness forced me to think clearly and who provided much needed and much appreciated stimulation, I give humble gratitude.

I wish to give specific thanks to several people who have been of special assistance to me. First, I would like to thank my graduate assistants Gerry Bode and Charles Henrickson for their careful research. I am grateful to John Johnson, president of Concordia Seminary, for his support and assistance in providing the opportunity to complete this project. I am grateful to Robert Kolb for his always welcome encouragement. I thank especially Charles Arand, a faithful friend and treasured colleague. I thank John Nunes, friend and editor in Christ.

Finally, I am grateful, more than I can say, to Sherry, my wife, my partner, my friend.

Introduction

> The Word became flesh and made His dwelling among us. We have seen His glory, the glory of the One and Only, who came from the Father, full of grace and truth. (John 1:14)

The Gospel is more than words. It is the dynamic, saving action of God in Christ Jesus through any of its various forms: Word or Sacrament. The Gospel is more than words, but it is still words—words about the Word made flesh for us, words that convey the Word made flesh to us. Is the Gospel just words? Hardly! But it is words nonetheless. It is words that convey and bestow the justification of God on sinners, apart from works of the law, by grace alone, through faith alone, for Christ's sake alone. Just words? No, *Just Words*.

This book will explore the wonderful variety of ways the Gospel comes in *words* and the language used by the biblical writers to describe and convey what God has done for us in Christ. This book is an attempt to investigate the language of the Gospel, to poke around into the Word as language, to feel the rich textures, to peer into the "inner world" of the words called the doctrine of justification. The purpose is to help all Christians not only to grasp and understand the Gospel, but also to proclaim and communicate it in its fullness, to hear it and say it in all its ways of being heard and said, through all God's beautiful words.

Part 1 focuses on the relationship between the Gospel and the doctrine of justification by grace through faith. It highlights the role this central doctrine plays in Christian theology. The chapters also explore the relationship between the Gospel as a divine Word and as human words. This section looks at the nature and function of words in general and the nature of the Word of God in particular. It focuses on rhetoric, particularly metaphor, as a necessary function of language, necessary because it advances our knowledge of reality.

Parts 2 through 7 explore six ways to say the Gospel or six "metaphors for the Gospel": creation, commerce, law, relationships, sacrifice, and deliverance. In each case, the metaphor is illustrated by means of a scenario in which the metaphor may profitably be used, an exposition of primary scriptural texts, and an exploration of the "problem" that lies behind the metaphor. Additional scriptural texts for further study and reflection on the metaphor are available in the appendix.

Part 8 examines the relationship between the universality of the Gospel and the universality of its words. It attempts to show that not only the substance but also the form of the Gospel is a way to reach beyond self, to transcend the particularities of denominational commonplaces and of culture and language. Thus, chapter 26 discusses the implications the metaphorical nature of the language of the Gospel has for evangelism. Better use of the rich language of the Gospel can be a way to cross the barriers that exist between people so "the Word may not be bound but have free course and be preached to the joy and edifying of Christ's holy people" (TLH, 14).

This book also explores the ecumenical and missiological implications of Gospel language, especially the importance that an understanding of the language of the Gospel as metaphor has for inter-Christian and inter-religious dialogue. To some extent, such an understanding enables us to talk with one another as Christians of differing confessions and to friends who are not Christians.

Several works have paved the way for this book and have informed my thinking to a greater or lesser degree. Leon Morris' excellent work, *The Apostolic Preaching of the Cross*,[1] is in many ways a landmark book. It has had a powerful influence on my thinking, which I happily acknowledge. Alister E. McGrath has written more on the subject of the Gospel than perhaps anyone else over the past decade. I am indebted especially to his *Iustitia Dei: A History of the Christian Doctrine of Justification,*[2] which helped me to gain historical perspective on the doctrine of justification. Richard Caemmerer's influential book, *Preaching for the Church,*[3] contains a list of the diverse types of language in which the Gospel is presented in Scripture. Finally, Colin Gunton's *The Actuality of Atonement*[4] is helpful not only because of its excellent exploration into the rhetorical, especially metaphorical, dimensions of language, but also in the way Gunton presents the nature and scope of the various metaphors, though in a very different way than the present volume. All of these books have been helpful, and I heartily recommend them for further study.

The ultimate purpose for writing this book is to hold before God's people the fullness of the biblical witness to the Gospel so the Scriptures may truly be a fount and source not only of faith and life, but also of the language to glorify Christ and to serve His people. Is the Gospel just words? No! Never just words. Rather, words that make us just.

ENDNOTES

1. Leon Morris, *The Apostolic Preaching of the Cross* (Grand Rapids: Wm. B. Eerdmans, 1984).

2. Alister E. McGrath, *Iustitia Dei: A History of the Christian Doctrine of Justification* (Cambridge: Cambridge University Press, 1989). Also helpful are McGrath's *Justification by Faith: What It Means for Us Today* (Grand Rapids: Academic Books, 1988), and *The Mystery of the Cross* (Grand Rapids: Academic Books, 1988).

3. Richard H. Caemmerer, *Preaching for the Church: Theology and Technique of the Christian Sermon* (St. Louis: Concordia Publishing House, 1959). See especially pages 330–331.

4. Colin E. Gunton, *The Actuality of Atonement: A Study of Metaphor, Rationality and the Christian Tradition* (Grand Rapids: Wm. B. Eerdmans, 1989).

PART 1

JUST WORDS

1

The Gospel
and Justification

I am not ashamed of the Gospel, because it is the power
of God for the salvation of everyone who believes: first
for the Jew, then for the Gentile. For in the Gospel a
righteousness from God is revealed, a righteousness
that is by faith from first to last, just as it is written:
"The righteous will live by faith." (Romans 1:16–17)

THE SCOPE OF THE GOSPEL

What is the Gospel? What exactly is the language of the
Gospel? How do we know when we have the Gospel, when we
have said it, when we have heard it? Above all, what is the relationship between the Gospel and what we call the "doctrine of
justification"?

The word *Gospel* means "good news." It derives from the
Greek word *euangelion,* which literally means "good message."
Gospel refers to the fact that God has Good News to proclaim
to His sinful creatures: Their sins are forgiven; they are declared
innocent because of the work of Jesus Christ, God's own Son,
on their behalf. The Gospel is Good News. As a message of

Good News, the Gospel can be and is used quite properly in a variety of ways.

First, the Gospel refers to those portions of the Scriptures that tell the story of Jesus. The biblical books of Matthew, Mark, Luke, and John are known as "gospels" because they were written for the express purpose of telling the Good News of God's provision for the salvation of human beings in the life, death, and resurrection of Jesus.

Second, we use the word *Gospel* to refer broadly to any revelation of God, regardless of the content. For example, some use the word *Gospel* not only to refer to what God has done for us in Christ, but also to refer to what God commands of us as a righteous and demanding God.[1]

Third, we use the word *Gospel* to refer specifically to the work of Jesus on our behalf. It is the Good News that God is reconciled to a world of sinners. This is the way it is used most commonly among the Reformers of the 16th century. They carefully separated what God has done for us in Jesus Christ from what God demands from us. The former they called the Gospel, the latter the Law. The Gospel is not what we do as a loving response to God's graciousness in Christ. This they usually referred to as sanctification. In a narrow, restricted sense, Gospel is what God has done for us in Jesus Christ to rescue us from our sin and to make us holy in His sight.

The Gospel as Word and Sacraments

Although a primary form of the Gospel is the words about Christ's saving work on our behalf, words are not the only form the Gospel takes. The Gospel, the "power of God for the salvation of everyone who believes" (Romans 1:16), comes in *verbal* and in *visible* forms. A person receives God's favor in the Gospel either by *hearing* the message proclaimed (in sermons, in Bible classes, or in other simple verbal expressions of God's love in Christ) or by receiving it through *visible* means—the water of Baptism or the bread and wine of the Lord's Supper.

The Gospel is verbal—conveyed through words—and it is visible in water and in bread and wine.

It must be clear from the outset that the Gospel is more than words. In whatever form, whether Word or sacraments, we hear and see and receive the same Gospel, the same saving power of God in Christ. Both Word and sacraments provide the same access to the favor and love of the heavenly Father. These wonderfully diverse forms of the Gospel should never be considered to be in competition with, or even contradictory to, each other. They are different ways our gracious God has provided to bestow on us the saving blessings earned by Christ on the cross.[2]

Further, these forms of the Gospel are not as separate as one might think. The sacraments are not merely materialistic rituals, external signs. They need the Word to give them power, to explain them, and to interpret them for our learning and benefit. Likewise, the Word is not a unidimensional, flat, interior, intellectual word. It is a dynamic, eventful Word that goes forth from God into the real world with powerful effects.

THE GOSPEL AS EVENTFUL WORD

The Gospel is more than words. In today's world, words tend to be flat, merely descriptive, without any real force. Although we love and defend our First Amendment rights to free speech, as a culture we generally have a low opinion of words and their power. Too often we actually believe the saying, "Sticks and stones may break my bones, but words will never hurt me." We think of words as less harmful, less powerful, than actions. We are dead wrong. In our hearts we know that words *do* hurt. Anyone who has been crushed by careless criticism or who has felt remorse over a "cutting word" knows that words have power. Words bite and break. Words kill.

When spoken or read, words make something happen. Communication through words is an event. This is true of any communication, but it is especially true of communication with the Gospel because the Gospel is the Word of God. The Word of God is a creative, powerful word, energized by the Holy Spirit. Both the Law (what God demands of us because of His perfection) and the Gospel (what God has done perfectly for us in His Son) are creative, powerful words. The Law creates sorrow in sinful hearts. The Gospel also creates. It creates true faith in the hearts of sinful people, something no ordinary word could do. Although all words are eventful, only the Word of God is fully creative and powerful. The Word of God is *theologically* eventful because in it God is at work doing what only He can do.

THE WORD OF GOD AND THE WORDS OF HUMANS

The Holy Spirit works powerfully and creatively in our hearts through the *Word* of Law and of Gospel. That is, the Holy Spirit speaks to us "in, with, and under" human expressions and human language. These two forms of creativity, God's and ours, do not work at cross purposes with each other and should not be seen as contradicting each other. To be sure, our creativity is only descriptive and evocative while God's is performative. In our use of words, we are like an artist who is restricted to the use of preexisting materials. The artist doesn't create anything new. He or she "creates" a new perspective of what already is there through the imaginative use of media, whether the reflective qualities of paint or film or metal. God's Word, on the other hand, is creative in a far more profound sense. It performs. It does what it says. As God says in Isaiah's prophecy:

> "As the rain and the snow come down from heaven, and do not return to it without watering the earth and making it bud and flourish, so that it yields seed for the sower and bread for the eater, so is My word that goes out from My mouth: It will not return to Me empty, but will accomplish what I desire and achieve the purpose for which I sent it." (Isaiah 55:10–11)

When God speaks, He brings into being things *ex nihilo* (out of nothing), as He did in the beginning (Genesis 1:1). God speaks into being things that are not. Just as in the beginning He said, "Let there be light," and light was, so today He says through the Gospel, "Let there be faith in the heart of a sinner," and faith is. This divine Word comes in human words, and it comes *only* through human words. These words of the Gospel are inspired by God the Holy Spirit. The Holy Spirit works creatively in the hearts of people even as we seek to speak the Gospel creatively to others.

A DIVINE AND HUMAN WORD

What is the nature of this relationship between God's Word and human words? An analogy can help illustrate the relationship. There is a connection between the Word Incarnate—the God-man, Jesus Christ—and the Word about the Word Incarnate, the Gospel.

Our Lord Jesus is both divine and human. He is God, and He is man. He has a divine nature and a human nature. There is something about Jesus that is divine and something that is human. Yet He is not *partly* divine and *partly* human, as if His divinity and His humanity could be separated from each other. Since His conception, the eternal Logos, the Second Person of the Trinity, has been united inseparably with His human nature in a mysterious but wonderful Personal Union.

It is a mystery: Jesus is *fully* and *genuinely* divine and at the same time *fully* and *genuinely* human. As God, Jesus is fully divine, and He possesses all the attributes of God. He is eternal, unchangeable, almighty, all-knowing, and is present everywhere. Jesus also has divine names and does the work of God. As human, He lacks nothing of genuine humanness, and He experiences all that our humanity includes (except sin). This great mystery has been believed and confessed by Christians through all the ages of the church: Jesus is "very God of very God ... born of the virgin Mary." This constitutes the orthodox teaching on who Christ is. Any view that diminishes or denies the completeness or genuineness of His divinity or of His humanity is an error that is harmful to faith.

The analogy with the Word of the Gospel is this: The Gospel Word also can be said to have two natures—divine and human. As a divine Word, it has certain divine qualities. The Gospel has divine power or efficacy—it can bring us to faith in Jesus. It has divine sufficiency—it is enough for our salvation. It has divine perfection—it is complete. To deny this nature of the Gospel is to rob it of something essential, something necessary for it to be *Gospel*. To deny this nature of the Gospel would be to make it into merely a flat and powerless human word, incapable of doing the divine work of snatching sinners from certain destruction and transferring them into the kingdom of heaven.

As a human word, on the other hand, the Gospel has certain human qualities as well: language, literary form, historical context, grammar, syntax, and rhetoric. To deny this nature of the Gospel is to rob it of something essential, something necessary for it to be *Gospel*. To deny this nature of the Gospel would be to make it into an a-historical, a-textual word that is incapable of conveying the divinely powerful Word of God in terms and categories humans can understand.

The Divine Solution to the Human Problem

It is helpful to clarify what the Gospel stands against, what it is *not*. The Gospel is the solution to the problem of the Law. In the divine Law, we see our ultimate concern before God. The Gospel is the Good News only if it comes as the solution to the problem of God—His wrath, His condemnation, His estrangement from us because of our sin. In a sense, the real human predicament is the reality of the God who judges, the reality of the God in the light of whose Law we stand accused. In the light of God's life, we are dead. In the light of God's perfection, we are defiled. Through the Law, we recognize who we are as we stand in God's presence.

The Law also points to the problem between people. Sin has a social, psychological, perhaps even a genetic, dimension. Primarily, however, our real "problem" is God. We need a solution to the problem of God, to the problem that *is* God. It may sound strange, even blasphemous, but our predicament as sinners is not merely that our sins are harmful to us and to our neighbors. The deeper truth is that God is angry and personally offended by our sins. God's anger and wrath need appeasement. In this sense, God is the true problem that needs to be solved. Our problem has a name: God.

The Gospel describes the solution to precisely this problem. This means that the language of the Gospel is, in the first instance, *theo*logical language. That is, the Gospel is language about God. It describes the relationship God has to us, specifically what God has done for us in Christ to solve this problem.[3] As a result of Christ's perfect obedience, God's wrath was turned away and He turned a favorable gaze toward us.

The Gospel always refers to the work of God in Christ. It tells what God has done in the historical events associated with the earthly ministry of Jesus Christ in first-century Palestine. It is, therefore, *extra nos* or *outside of us.* The focus of the Gospel is always on Christ.

The Gospel also refers to the work God did *pro nobis,* or *for us,* in the historical actions of Christ on the cross. We rejoice in what God is doing in those whom He justifies, but this is the "fruit," or result, of the Gospel—that is, sanctification—and not the Gospel itself.

The Gospel stresses the sole sufficiency of Christ's work on behalf of the world on Good Friday and Easter. It is the Word of God located specifically and narrowly in Christ's obedience—active in His living and passive in His dying. This Good News was consummated at the cross and announced victoriously at the resurrection of our Lord. The Reformers used the phrase *solo Christo* (*Christ alone*), to identify this particular nuance of the Gospel.

The Gospel also recognizes and honors the fact that our favorable standing before God exists solely because of His grace. This concept is described in the phrase *sola gratia* (*grace alone*). Gospel language, therefore, gives all credit for our salvation to God in Christ and not to God's transforming work in us, to our faith, or to our good works and love.

Finally, the Gospel acknowledges that a person's salvation is brought about through *faith alone* (*sola fide*). Faith is the means of receiving the benefits of Christ's work on the cross. Faith is not a "cause" of salvation.[4] We are not saved because of our faith. We are redeemed through faith as a means of receiving the final and perfect redemption worked out by Christ. Only in this way does Christ receive all the glory for our salvation. Only in this way do we poor sinners receive maximum comfort from our salvation.

THE GOSPEL AND THE DOCTRINE OF JUSTIFICATION

Reformation theology affirms the doctrine of justification as the article on which the church stands or falls. This is the Gospel! For the church's continuing existence, the message of the Gospel must remain in place: that sinners are holy before God by grace, for Christ's sake, through faith alone, apart from works of the law.

The doctrine of justification is really the Gospel itself. This Gospel stands *over* the church as the criterion of the church's authenticity. It is the judge of what is truly the church and what is not. It is the presence of this Gospel in its verbal and visible forms that identifies the church of Jesus Christ and distinguishes it from every other organization or sect. Where this Gospel is, we have the church. Where we do not have evidence of this Gospel, we do not have visible or trustworthy evidence of the church.

The Gospel also stands *under* the church as its only firm foundation. Without the Gospel, the church cannot stand for one hour. It is the substance of the faith—the substratum, the fundament—on which theology, the church, and faith stand. Without the foundation of the Gospel, we fall. We simply lose everything.

MORE THAN ONE WAY TO SAY IT

How do we say the doctrine of justification? What words do we use? Do we claim too much when we insist that the doctrine of justification is the article on which the church stands and falls? Is justification one way of saying the Gospel? Some might respond that justification is merely "your way of saying the Gospel." Some claim different people have different ways to speak about God and salvation.

We use the word *justification* in two different, yet related, ways.[5]

The Bible uses the words *justify* and *justification* to refer to God's saving work among humankind. It is legal, or forensic, language. Such language is especially common in Paul's letters. We also use the word *justification* in a broader way to denote the doctrine of justification as distinct from the doctrine of sanctification or any other article of faith.[6] In this sense, that is synecdochally,[7] the doctrine of justification is more than the legal language. It stands in for all the ways of saying the Gospel and includes all the words—all the rich and variegated language—of the Gospel. In terms of language, justification is *one* of the words. In terms of doctrine, it contains *all* the words—all the ideas—within itself and cannot be reduced merely to one or two words.

The legal, or forensic, language *is* essential. That language articulates something about the Gospel that is both biblical and necessary. Any conception of the Gospel that ignores or eliminates the legal imagery is flawed, perhaps fatally. In fact, the great contribution of the Reformation was this truth about salvation: God justifies the guilty. The medieval church lacked the objective, forensic emphasis of salvation in Christ. Nevertheless, when we say that God justifies the guilty, we have not said all there is to say about salvation.

Each Gospel word, phrase, and idea is necessary to the fullness of the biblical doctrine of justification. Every Gospel word contributes something distinctive, something unique, which, if it were not present, would make the doctrine less than whole, less than fully what the Lord revealed.

The failure to understand and appreciate the fullness of the Gospel has led to errors throughout the history of theology concerning the doctrine of justification. Often culture and context so influence church theologians that they allow a single metaphor to dominate the discussion or interpretation of Christ's work of salvation. For example, in feudal times, commercial metaphors dominated. This led to a conception of the Gospel in primarily monetary terms. This, in turn, led to such errors as the "treasure of merits" and the buying and selling of forgiveness through the sale of indulgences.

The goal is not to reduce the Gospel to one of its words, but to proclaim it in its fullness, to use all its ways of being said. The goal is, in addition to proclaiming the Gospel as a divine, powerful Word, to proclaim it as a profound and richly textured human word.

ENDNOTES

1. Although the word *Gospel* may be used in a broader sense, serious misunderstanding results from referring to what the righteous God demands of poor miserable sinners as "good news." It is important to define carefully theological language, especially when we refer to God's act of saving us in Christ.

2. When people pit these two forms of the Gospel against each other, the result is always sad and sometimes tragic. Some raise the Word over the sacraments as a more "pure" form of the Gospel. This may be a subtle form of rationalism, which sees the realm of ideas as a better and holier medium for the Gospel. On the other hand, by exalting sacraments over the Word, we also undermine the Gospel. The solution is obvious: Both Word and

sacraments are equally honored by us and are given the highest place in our theology and life as gifts from the Lord who instituted both.

3. St. Paul masterfully makes this point in Romans 3.

4. Some theologians speak of faith as a *cause* of justification. They are, generally, careful to identify faith as an *instrumental cause,* emphasizing the fact that faith is the instrument through which we receive God's grace. The true cause of our justification before God is the gracious will of God and the saving work of Christ.

5. See my essay "Justification by Faith: The *Articulus Stantis et Cadentis Ecclesiae,*" in *And Every Tongue Confess: Essays in Honor of Norman Nagel,* ed. by Gerald S. Krispin and Jon P. Vieker (Dearborn, MI: Nagel Festschrift Committee, 1990), 264–282.

6. This is the way the Lutheran Confessions use the word *justification,* often in parallel with other biblical words for the Gospel.

7. Synecdoche is a rhetorical device whereby the "whole thing" is intended by reference simply to a part. See page 31.

2

The Gospel as Words

But now He has reconciled you by Christ's physical body through death to present you holy in His sight, without blemish and free from accusation—if you continue in your faith, established and firm, not moved from the hope held out in the Gospel. This is the Gospel that you heard and that has been proclaimed to every creature under heaven, and of which I, Paul, have become a servant. (Colossians 1:22–23)

JUSTIFICATION BY ANY OTHER NAME

Centuries ago, Shakespeare penned the famous lines:

> What's in a name? that which we call a rose
> By any other name would smell as sweet.[1]

Yet names have the power to identify, clarify, and describe. To have someone's name is to have the person.

What name do we give to this "rose" known as the doctrine of justification? What language do we use to say the sweet message of the Gospel? The Bible gives us a deep and rich language, one laden with colorful metaphors that speak of the wonderful things our God has done for us in Christ Jesus. We have many ways to say the truth of justification, many names to give it. Each delivers its own share of the truth of God's love for us.

Pastors who preach the Gospel every week and believers who desire to tell friends and relatives about Jesus Christ often tire of saying or hearing the Gospel in the "same old way." Much of the language seems antiquated. The concepts seem foreign and unusual to 21st-century minds. The Gospel has an aura of "churchliness," of otherworldliness, that, frankly, sounds strange in the ears of modern people.

Christians often get the idea that to make the Gospel more palatable or exciting we must create new categories, new forms of language, new images that better reflect what's happening in the world. These new categories, insofar as they accurately reflect what Scripture says about God's saving action in Christ, may help to make the Gospel more intelligible. Yet the primary task is not to come up with *new* ways to say the Gospel, but to return to and revitalize the *old* ways to say it.

Scripture is a veritable gold mine of terms and metaphors that are vivid and descriptive of God's love in Christ. Furthermore, these words and phrases are sanctioned by the inspired writers of sacred Scripture. The holy writers used these words to describe the results of Christ's justifying work. Teachers and preachers of the Word have used such scriptural language throughout all the ages of the church. There is a solidity and substance to these biblical words that new categories or metaphors for the Gospel do not possess. Whether in the Bible or conveyed in classic theological works, liturgies, or devotional works, the Gospel words and phrases of Scripture protect us from the errors to which more time-bound metaphors may be susceptible. Their familiarity, however, also may cause us to take them for granted and may lead to a failure to appreciate them as powerful, evocative, and living metaphors.

THE REALITY OF THE GOSPEL

The word *metaphor* describes this biblical language of the Gospel. What does it mean, though, to talk about Gospel and metaphor? First, metaphor does not mean that the Gospel is unreal or mythical or symbolic or representational or anything else that would erode its power for the salvation of the world.[2] Christ is, and was during His earthly ministry, *real*. God's incarnation is real. Christ's work is real. The benefits of His work for us are real. God really did become incarnate—come in the flesh—in the person of Jesus of Nazareth.

This God/Man really did live, serve, suffer, die, and rise from the dead, just as the Scriptures say. The effects of His work on our behalf are real, actual, historical. In fact, it is on this reality, this solidity, this one foundation, that our entire faith rests. This is the reality on which the church stands and falls. From this reality arises the reality of Christ's promise and presence for us in the sacraments and the Word.

God is not a metaphor; He is real. The descriptions we have of God in Scripture are not metaphorical.[3] God really is *Father*, though in a way far deeper and more perfect than we have ever seen or can imagine. God is truly *Father*, as the Bible says, and this is a meaningful statement. However, He is not *Father* in the same sense that we experience fatherhood because we are sinful and finite. God is *Father* in a fuller, more complete sense, in an infinite sense that we never can know fully. Although fatherhood as we know it is analogous to the way God is Father, it is not identical to it in every respect.

How do we spell out the implications for us today of Christ's life, suffering, death, and resurrection? How do we articulate the benefits of Christ's real, historical actions for all the world for all time? The facts of history are *literally* true. But much of the language we use to explain the facts of history is metaphorical.

Despite this extensive discussion of metaphor, there has been no simple definition of *metaphor*. Definitions abound.

Differences of opinion exist even among the experts. Furthermore, it is not always easy to distinguish a metaphor from some of its semantic cousins, including simile, analogy, synecdoche, catachresis, and metonymy. It is not possible to enter into a full discussion of language here. Nevertheless, a brief definition of metaphor and the other figures of speech is necessary.[4]

Words Left to Their Own (Rhetorical) Devices

Simile

A simile is the rhetorical device that is most similar, at least in a superficial sense, to a metaphor. It is usually regarded as a simple comparison of one thing to another, and it includes the words "like" or "as." An example of a simile is "Sherry is like a rose." The comparison sheds light on the subject: Sherry is, by means of this simile, seen to be beautiful, delicate, sweet-smelling, and so forth. Of course, Sherry remains Sherry and the rose remains the rose. Not all of a rose's components transfer well to Sherry. For example, Sherry does not have thorns that prick, does not go dormant in autumn, and is not susceptible to mites.

A simile often uses a subject that is reasonably well-known to explain something that is impossible for humans to fully understand, such as when we say that light is like waves. Our common knowledge of waves helps us to more fully understand the nature of light, a phenomenon that is less commonly known to us.[5]

Analogy

The term *analogy* signifies several things. It can refer to a type of relationship, such as when we say that membership in the church is analogous to a marriage between husband and wife (Ephesians 5). Analogy also can designate a kind of argument (based on the kind of analogy just suggested). It is, however, *linguistic* analogy that is of particular interest for Scripture. Analogy is a linguistic device whereby language is "stretched" to fit new applications. Thus, a word retains a central core of meaning but also comes to have a wider range of application. For example, though once appropriate to horses, *riding* is now used in reference to bicycles or cars.[6] An analogy is different from a metaphor because from its inception, an analogy is appropriate, but a metaphor appears shocking at first. Metaphor is a greater "stretch" than analogy. More components of meaning naturally transfer in an analogy than in a metaphor. There is much greater correspondence between two things that are analogous than when metaphor is employed.

SYNECDOCHE

Synecdoche is a rhetorical device whereby one moves from genus to species or vice versa.[7] In other words, we refer to the whole by naming a part or we refer to a part by naming the whole. For example, "The ships opened fire" really means "The guns on the ship opened fire." In synecdoche, we mention the whole while intending a part.[8] On the other hand, if we say, "The hearts of all people are sinful," we do not mean that only the heart (and not any other part) is sinful. In this example, we use synecdoche—naming a part but intending the whole.

METONYMY

Metonymy is similar to synecdoche. Metonymy means giving a thing a name that belongs to one of its attributes.[9] In other words, we use an adjunct to stand for the whole. When the newspaper reports, "The White House said yesterday ...," it really means, "The President said yesterday ...." *White House* is an attribute (the residence, office, etc.) of the president.[10]

CATACHRESIS

Catachresis gives a thing that lacks a proper name a name that belongs to something else. It is a type of metaphor that supplies a term where one is lacking in the vocabulary. This is how the base of a mountain became known as the "foot" or the item on which the text of a book appears became known as a "leaf." In other words, catachresis "is the activity of filling lexical gaps."[11]

THE MEANING OF *Metaphor*

We have come full circle to the definition of *metaphor*, the richest and most powerful of all rhetorical devices. Perhaps Aristotle's classic definition is a good place to begin: Metaphor is "the application of an alien name by transference."[12] In other words, a term belonging somewhere else is used in an unusual context, as when we say, "Sherry is a rose"; "Time is a thief"; or "Christ's death on the cross is a victory."[13]

Notice the difference between a metaphor and a simile. A simile would say: "Sherry is *like* a rose"; "Time is like a thief"; or "Christ's death on the cross is *like* a victory." Similes communicate a much softer comparison. A simile involves the transference of fewer components of meaning. A simile seems to highlight not only which aspects of "cross" and "victory" are similar, but also which are different. It leaves both "cross" and "victory" unchanged.

Metaphor, on the other hand, invites a more penetrating comparison, almost an identification. In fact, a metaphor blurs the distinction between "cross" and "victory" to the point where the words begin to take on a meaning they did not have prior to their juxtaposition in the metaphor. The metaphor "creates new meaning" as neither "cross" nor "victory" is left unchanged in the process. Both are seen in a new light because they were placed together by the metaphor.[14]

A metaphor is something done to and with language, or as Nelson Goodman has suggested in highly metaphorical language: "Metaphor is teaching an old word new tricks," or metaphor is "an affair between a predicate with a past and an object that yields while protesting."[15] Perhaps a good working definition of a metaphor would be: "A metaphor is a figure of speech whereby we speak about one thing in terms which are seen to be suggestive of another."[16]

A metaphor is a verbal convention, a rhetorical device. But it is more than mere "word games," and it is certainly not an abuse of language. It used to be a common belief that a metaphor was basically a lie. For example, to say that a "cross" is a "victory" is a lie because we all know that a cross *literally* is not a victory. It is a bloody and horrible death and a defeat. One still hears this disparagement of metaphor as only a "rhetorical device" or as "merely a word game" as opposed to what is literal and real.

Now, however, many linguists and theologians offer a more positive assessment of the literary or rhetorical dimensions of language. In fact, there is a lively connection between metaphor and reality. As Thomas Long says, "The literary dimensions of texts are not merely decorative."[17] He further suggests that rather than thinking of the form and content of language as two separate realities, it would be more accurate to think of "the form of the content."[18]

In fact, some social scientists today hold that there can be no progress in our knowledge of the world without the development of metaphors or other figures of speech. We comprehend aspects of the world only as we find new words to use in our search for understanding.[19] Metaphor is, therefore, necessary for the advancement of knowledge.

When we learn a new thing, we may say, "I see it now." This phrase means we have connected in some way the new thing with what we already know. We have made an association between what is known and what is unknown. Thus, we construct knowledge by building on what we already know. We really cannot learn or understand new things except through some sort of connection or association.[20]

Walter Ong, a prominent literary critic, makes the point that judgment is always binary. We can grasp nothing in itself but only as it is related to and set apart from something else.[21] Because they relate what is known to what is unknown, metaphors make it possible for us to advance in our knowledge of reality.

The point is this: Metaphors convey truth. While most metaphors are at least partly false because their statements do not correspond literally with the truth (though it could be argued that there are no statements that are literally true in this sense), what they convey is (or certainly can be) true. For example, consider this: "Watch out! That's a live wire!" You could, of course, respond, "Well, that's only metaphorically true. Wires are not 'alive.' " But if you touched the wire, you would soon find out the truth about *dead* and *alive*. The statement that the wire is "alive" is true, but it is expressed metaphorically.[22] Thus metaphors are "referential"; they refer, in figurative language, to realities.

So it is with the biblical language of the Gospel. It is true—it refers to historical realities—but it is expressed metaphorically. In fact, there is no way to say the Gospel and spell out the implications of the Gospel without words, without metaphors. Our problem is that we have forgotten—or perhaps we never even knew—that our language is metaphorical. What we sometimes see as literal usage actually is often metaphorical. Both ordinary and technical language is filled with usages that we assume were originally metaphorical, such as "*neck* of the bottle," "*leaf* of the book," "*flow* of electricity." However, we now have no figurative connotations for these metaphors for the native speaker. We call these dead metaphors.[23]

LIVING METAPHORS!

To explain what God did for us in Christ, the biblical writers, under the inspiration of the Holy Spirit, borrowed language from other contexts: creation, commerce, law, relationships, sacrifice, and deliverance. The Scriptures say that in Christ we are enlightened, we are reborn, we are redeemed, we are justified, we are reconciled, we are hallowed, we are delivered, we are saved, and we are forgiven. We tend to hear all these as virtually synonymous, as indeed they are when we speak doctrinally. But in their linguistic meaning, such phrases are not synonymous. They are metaphors that have died, that have become lifeless, because of frequent use (and abuse). Each word, each metaphor, waits to be raised to life.

Colin Gunton has written that preaching the Word "continues to be testimony both to the capacity of words to be living, to make things happen, and to the mode of the divine victory which is 'not by might, nor by power, but by my Spirit...' The word is mightier than the sword, as both cross and resurrection avow."[24] There is a twofold nature to the life of the Word of the Gospel. First, it is alive as the Word of God, which is energized by the Holy Spirit, who, in and through the words, does the divine and miraculous work of bringing sinners to a conviction of their sinfulness and prompts them to turn to Christ in faith. The Spirit-drenched Word of the Gospel frees Jesus from the past and makes His victory over death at the cross alive in the lives of those who hear it today. The Gospel is alive because the Spirit energizes and vivifies it.

The Gospel also is alive simply because it is words. It is alive with words and metaphors that are themselves living. These words actually make things happen. Everyone experiences the power of words: to destroy or to build up, to bring tears of sadness or of joy, to strengthen or to weaken, to comfort or to cause distress, to encourage or to discourage, and to disturb or to calm. Words as words, simply because they are words, have power. They are alive.

This power is particularly evident in metaphors. Good metaphors are vivid and evocative. In fact, each way of saying the Gospel is a figure of speech whereby we speak about one true thing in terms that are seen to be suggestive of another. It is metaphor, at least as language. It is metaphor precisely because it is language.

Francis Rossow writes:

Once God in His wisdom committed Himself to language as a means to communicate His saving love, He simultaneously committed Himself to the use of metaphor. When words are used, metaphor is inevitable. I hasten to add that this outcome is not at all unfortunate. It is cause for rejoicing. Our language is the richer for it. Metaphor helps rather than hinders communication. In brief, metaphor is a necessary good.[25]

Instead of hearing and communicating the Gospel with the richness and vividness that each metaphor contains within it, we tend to blend language together. We generalize metaphors and flatten them out so they all end up meaning virtually the same thing. We wind up with the doctrinal nutrients, but we lose the distinctive flavors of the language.

THE WORLD INSIDE THE WORDS

Each word, each metaphor, has a world inside of it. Each has a particular way of referring to or conceptualizing our standing before God. Metaphors have their own internal worldview into which the skillful preacher or communicator invites hearers. Inside the metaphor is a universe, a richly textured and beautifully colored reality through which the hearer of the Word is invited to view himself or herself. Through this universe, we understand, even visualize, how God is toward us on account of Christ.

To blend all metaphors together, to take off the sharp edges of the various metaphors, may be something like the following:

Imagine ordering a nine-course dinner. The green salad is cool and crisp, the soup clear and tasty. The brightly colored vegetables are steamed just right. The steak and lobster are cooked to perfection. Flaky bread, soft and warm, is served with creamy butter. A bottle of fine wine complements the entree. Sweet dessert follows with rich black coffee. What a delightful experience! With so many colors, flavors, textures, temperatures, the meal is complete.

Then imagine asking the waiter to throw all the courses into a blender and turn the knob to purée. What would become of the dinner's attractiveness? What color would it be now? What would be its texture, its flavor, its temperature? It would come out colorless, bland, runny, and lukewarm at best. It would be totally unpalatable. You would lose your appetite immediately. You would push it away from you, turn your back on it, and walk away from the table as quickly as possible.

Of course, no one would ever think of doing such a thing. Yet in a way, that's what we do with the Gospel when we blend together all the beautiful words, the vivid metaphors, and proclaim them in a flat, bland, runny way. No wonder people tire of hearing the "same old thing" over and over again. No wonder preachers burn out on preaching or succumb to the temptation of creating a "new gospel," something more innovative and creative. No wonder we despair of being able to communicate the Gospel to our family or friends in a clear, relevant, exciting way. What a sad state of affairs when Christians push the Gospel away, consider it unpalatable, turn their backs on it, and leave the table. How tragic when they tire of hearing the Gospel, when it seems flat, bland, boring, and dead!

MINING THE TREASURES OF THE GOSPEL

The following chapters whet the appetite to the wealth and richness implicit in the language of the Gospel. They are confined to a study of the words that convey the doctrine of justification, as distinct from the doctrine of sanctification (or any other doctrine). It is little more than an introduction to the topic and serves to point the way toward a fuller apprehension of the Gospel as words. For the purposes of this study, the metaphors are primarily New Testament metaphors. Of course, the background of these metaphors is found in the Old Testament, which itself is rich in vivid language.

The chapters consist of groups or families (or semantic fields) of Gospel metaphors. This is not a comprehensive list. It is merely the current state of my penetration into the treasury of words provided by the Bible. The list seems to grow all the time as I discover new and exciting ways to say the Gospel, fresh ways to speak of the implications of the work of Christ, or what is called *soteriology*.

Through this careful examination of the biblical metaphors of the Gospel, we will not only understand them better, but articulate them, preach them, and speak them better and more creatively so Christ's name may be praised and His people blessed. Mining the verbal treasures of the Bible can be fun and rewarding.

ENDNOTES

1. William Shakespeare, *Romeo and Juliet,* II, ii, lines 43–44.
2. I do not mean, as some theologians do, that Christ's incarnation and saving ministry are metaphorical. Metaphor applies to language, not historical events. The Gospel, in its use of words, is metaphorical.
3. All language about God, that is, *theological* language, is of necessity analogical. While it is truly descriptive of God and relates how He truly is, it does not relate how He *fully* is. Finite human language, while able to convey true statements about the infinite God, cannot convey Him fully. The orthodox theologians used to speak about theological language as analogical, that is, related to analogy.
4. The literature on this topic is vast and growing. Especially helpful works include Colin Gunton, *The Actuality of Atonement: A Study of Metaphor, Rationality and the Christian Tradition* (Grand Rapids: Wm. B. Eerdmans, 1989) and Janet Martin Soskice, *Metaphor and Religious Language* (Oxford: Clarendon Press, 1985). Also helpful in the discussion are such works as George Aichele Jr., *The Limits of Story* (Philadelphia: Fortress Press, 1985); Rodney Kennedy, *The Creative Power of Metaphor: A Rhetorical Homiletics* (Lanham, Md.: University Press of America, 1993); Peter W. Macky, *The Centrality of Metaphors to Biblical Thought: A Method for Interpreting the Bible* (Lewiston, NY: The Edwin Mellen Press, 1990); John MacQuarrie, *God-Talk: An Examination of the Language and Logic of Theology* (New York: Harper & Row, 1967); Moises Silva, *God, Language, and Scripture: Reading the Bible in the Light of General Linguistics* (Grand Rapids: Zondervan, 1990); Richard Swinburne, *Revelation: From Metaphor to Analogy* (Oxford: Clarendon Press, 1992).

5. See Janet Martin Soskice, *Metaphor and Religious Language* (Oxford: Clarendon Press, 1985), 58–61; and C. M. Turbayne, *The Myth of Metaphor*, 2d ed. (Columbia: University of South Carolina Press, 1970), 11.

6. See *Metaphor and Religious Language,* 64–66.

7. *The Myth of Metaphor,* 11.

8. *Metaphor and Religious Language,* 57.

9. *The Myth of Metaphor,* 11.

10. *Metaphor and Religious Language,* 57. Synecdoche and metonymy may be said to be primarily ornamental or decorative. Metaphor goes beyond this. Metaphor actually makes something new.

11. Ibid., 61. While this technically may be called a metaphor, it is a simple kind of metaphor. While a metaphor borrows a name for a new thing from an old thing, it also creates new categories of meaning and actually advances knowledge, rather than merely giving names to known things that don't yet have them.

12. *Poetics,* 1457b, 7–8.

13. Colin E. Gunton, *The Actuality of Atonement: A Study of Metaphor, Rationality and the Christian Tradition* (Grand Rapids: Wm. B. Eerdmans, 1989), 28.

14. Ibid., 30. Gunton notes that no advance in knowledge is possible without the use and development of metaphors.

15. Ibid., 28.

16. *Metaphor and Religious Language,* 15.

17. Thomas G. Long, *Preaching and the Literary Forms of the Bible* (Philadelphia: Fortress Press, 1990), 12.

18. Ibid., 13.

19. *The Actuality of Atonement,* 31.

20. Sallie McFague, *Metaphorical Theology: Models of God* (Philadelphia: Fortress Press, 1997), 33.

21. Walther J. Ong, "Metaphor and the Twinned Vision," in *The Barbarian within and Other Fugitive Essays and Studies* (New York: Macmillan Co., 1962), 42.

22. *Metaphor and Religious Language,* 70.

23. Ibid., 71.

24. *The Actuality of Atonement,* 178.

25. Francis Rossow, *Preaching the Creative Gospel Creatively* (St. Louis: Concordia Publishing House, 1983), 34.

PART 2

CHRIST THE LIFE-GIVER:
CREATION METAPHORS

3

Birth

Praise be to the God and Father of our Lord Jesus
Christ! In His great mercy He has given us new birth
into a living hope through the resurrection of Jesus
Christ from the dead. (1 Peter 1:3)

A New Birth, a Living Hope

Lori and David were devastated. They had been given no
hint that anything was wrong. They never thought anything
like this could happen. Their first child, a little girl, was dead.

After a long, painful labor and delivery, Lori and David's
baby had been born six weeks premature. They named her
Hope, but she lived only a few minutes before dying from a
congenital birth defect. Lori and David's pastor baptized the
newborn moments before she died, which brought some comfort, but they still hurt beyond telling. The fleetingness and
fragility of life pressed in on them to the point that, at times,
they thought there was no hope.

In a Bible study at their church several weeks later, Lori
and David's pastor casually referred to 1 Peter 1:3: "[God] has
given us new birth into a living hope." Lori and David were
stunned—and thrilled. Never before had they heard the Gospel in such clear, relevant terms. *New birth. Living hope.* It now

made sense: Hope was alive. In that moment, they began the recovery from overwhelming grief and loss. Lori and David found the strength, by God's grace, to make a new beginning.

Born Again

One of the most vivid and perhaps most strange metaphors for the Gospel is birth and rebirth. Coming to faith in Jesus and receiving His life-giving benefits is a birth, is a rebirth—or better, is being born *anew*—by the power of God.

In ancient Greek mythology, the gods regularly came down from Mount Olympus and mingled with human beings. Some even had intercourse with mortals. The children born from these unions, both divine and human, often shared the character and attributes of the gods. These stories, of course, are crass expressions of the human longing for the divine. The biblical picture of God, the transcendent and infinite Creator, does not allow any kind of reckless interaction between God and His sinful and finite creatures. Yet Scripture speaks of those who have faith in Jesus Christ as those who have been "born again" or even "born of God." (See John 1:18; 1 John 3:9; 4:7; 5:1.)

Jesus Himself develops this metaphor of birth. He tells Nicodemus, a member of the Jewish ruling council, "I tell you the truth, no one can see the kingdom of God unless he is born again" (John 3:3). Nicodemus' reaction is revealing. Although he is no slouch intellectually, he does not understand that Jesus is speaking metaphorically. "How can a man be born when he is old?" he replies. "Surely he cannot enter a second time into his mother's womb to be born!" (John 3:4). Jesus then elaborates on His theme: "I tell you the truth, no one can enter the kingdom of God unless he is born of water and the Spirit. Flesh gives birth to flesh, but the Spirit gives birth to spirit" (John 3:5–6).

Why the birth metaphor? What is Jesus saying? Clearly He is saying that one enters into the kingdom of God (one enters into a favorable relationship with the Father) through a rebirth, a starting over again, which comes by water and the Spirit. Only the Spirit of God can do this. Our sinful flesh only generates what is of the flesh. We contribute as little to our spiritual birth as we do to our physical birth: nothing.[1] Even with this clarification, Nicodemus does not seem to understand. Jesus' metaphor has sufficient shock value to surprise Nicodemus. It does what any good metaphor is supposed to do. It makes a person think and grow by speaking of something unknown (how a person enters into the kingdom of God) in terms that are known (how a person enters the world). A metaphor generates both thought and knowledge, often because of its surprising qualities.

> For you have been born again, not of perishable seed, but of imperishable, through the living and enduring word of God. For, "All men are like grass, and all their glory is like the flowers of the field; the grass withers and the flowers fall, but the word of the Lord stands forever." And this is the word that was preached to you. (1 Peter 1:23–25)

As Those Unborn

Jesus announces simply and without hesitation that a person enters the kingdom of God by being born again by water and the Spirit. God causes us to be reborn. He "rebirths" us or gives birth to us. To what reality does this come as good news? What is the Law behind this rich Gospel?[2]

Many people experience life as a dead end. They see no purpose for their existence on earth, no reason to make it through the day. They don't know why they were born. Some feel they should never have been born. Their lives are adrift, meaningless, unformed, chaotic, unfocused. One all-too-common solution is to sever contact with reality through the abuse of drugs or alcohol.

Other people feel that they were "untimely born," that they are living in the wrong time. They long to go back to a better time and place or even all the way back into their mother's womb. Life is—and has been—hard. They've faced too many obstacles, endured too many setbacks. They go through life wishing for a "golden age" when things were simpler and life was kinder.

Both types of people need to know why they feel this way *theologically*. They need help to interpret their feelings and to understand their problem from God's perspective. Often the problem is not that they have lost a sense of meaning to life, but that they have lost *the* meaning of life. When we do not live in a faith relationship with God, or when we lose sight of God's call on our life, we cannot understand the ultimate purpose in our lives. We cannot see the purpose in our existence. Our real problem, then, is that we are cut off from what makes life worth living. We are searching for something or someone to explain life and enable us to put one foot in front of the other when times get tough.

David and Lori struggled with this question of meaning; they could see no purpose, no significance, in what happened to their baby. They couldn't accept her death. They wanted to return to a time before this tragedy. They didn't want to go on with their lives. They had no hope.

A New Beginning!

When David and Lori heard the Gospel, though, they discovered hope for the future. It came, ironically, in the form of rebirth "by water and the Spirit." They received comfort in knowing that Hope was baptized and so had been given the rebirth into new life. Her sins had been washed away, and she was given entrance into the kingdom of heaven. Lori and David were reminded of their own Baptism and the new beginning God had given them. Now, despite their tragedy, they had a new and living hope for their future. In one sense, they were able to begin their life together in Christ anew.

> At one time we too were foolish, disobedient, deceived and enslaved by all kinds of passions and pleasures. We lived in malice and envy, being hated and hating one another. But

when the kindness and love of God our Savior appeared, He saved us, not because of righteous things we have done, but because of His mercy. He saved us through the washing of rebirth and renewal by the Holy Spirit, whom he poured out on us generously through Jesus Christ our Savior, so that, having been justified by His grace, we might become heirs having the hope of eternal life. (Titus 3:3–7)

That's what the Gospel spoken in this way can do for us. Although Christ may not reveal to us the rhyme and reason for the things that happen to us, He enables us to see that we live in Him. Our lives are not meaningless. Although we may not always be able to discern it, God has a purpose for our lives. The ultimate solution to the problems and tragedies of life lies not in the past. It is not a matter of returning to the womb or to a better time. Nor does the solution come from altering one's sense of reality through drugs or alcohol or suicide.

Our life in Christ is lived out of the rebirth God gave us in our Baptism. In a very real way, we look backward every day as we remember our Baptism. We acknowledge that through water and the Word we have been united with Christ's death and resurrection. But the daily call of those who have been reborn, who have been given a new beginning in Christ, is to the present and the future. We grow in our perception of that new thing God has done with us. We increase in our ability to see the sense of the things that happen to us. Most of all, we look to that new day when the new birth we have now by faith will be made manifest in the perfection and life of the new kingdom in heaven.

ENDNOTES

1. Ewald Pless, *What Luther Says: A Practical In-Home Anthology for the Active Christian* (St. Louis: Concordia Publishing House, 1959), 344.
2. *Law* is a biblical word with broader implications than legal status and contexts. Although a legal term, Law also denotes the *problem* we have as sinners who stand before God. Like the word *justification*, Law can be used in a narrow sense to designate our "legal" standing before God or in a broad sense to describe *all* the ways we experience the problem of sin.

JUST WORDS

4

Life

"I am the resurrection and the life. He who believes in Me will live, even though he dies; and whoever lives and believes in Me will never die." (John 11:25)

A Matter of Life and Death

As Alma looked at Clarence's body, she wished that she were the one lying in the coffin. How could she go on? What would be the point?

For 47 years, Clarence had been an inseparable part of Alma's life. She had been devoted to him. She had defined herself in relation to him. For as long as she could remember, she had been "Clarence's wife." That's the way it was at church. That's the way it always had been when they were with his buddies from the shop. The only time she felt fully herself was when she was with Clarence. She could not imagine life without him, and she was not sure that she wanted to try. She just wanted to die.

Alma also felt guilty for having these feelings. She knew that she shouldn't think this way, but she simply didn't want to go on living without Clarence. During the funeral service, her pastor said something that Alma didn't quite hear. Days later, at the kitchen table where she and Clarence had sat each

49

morning and drank coffee, she sat quietly with the bulletin from the funeral service. A part of the sermon text was printed inside: "He who believes in Me will live, even though he dies; and whoever lives and believes in Me will never die."

Alma realized that though Clarence was dead *physically*, he was really still living. She was comforted by the knowledge that Clarence was, in the most important sense, alive in Christ and that she would see him again. She also began to think about her own situation. Although her life was a living death without Clarence, Alma became aware that she still shared her life in Christ with Clarence. That gave her courage and strength to endure the grief. With the help of her Christian friends, Alma began a new life, looking forward to a glorious reunion with Clarence in heaven.

The Resurrection and the Life

At first glance, we may not think of *life* as a metaphor for the Gospel. We hear about life, new life, and eternal life so often in sermons, Bible studies, and Christian books that we may think of this cluster of words *literally*, without any metaphorical overtones. In one sense, life is basic or fundamental to our Christian faith. But it is a metaphor. We borrow the word from the realm of creation so we can understand the implications of Christ's death and resurrection. Just as in the beginning God spoke life into being in His first creatures, so also He speaks life into being through the Word of Life, Jesus Christ. In beautiful and vivid imagery, life metaphors convey what God has done for us because of Christ.

The prologue to John's Gospel states this theme most forcefully:

> In the beginning was the Word, and the Word was with God, and the Word was God. He was with God in the beginning. Through Him all things were made; without Him nothing was made that has been made. In Him was life, and that life was the light of men. (John 1:1–4)

The connection between God's original creation—"in the beginning"—and God's re-creation in Christ is explicit. The means God uses in both cases is the same: the Word. In the beginning God gave life through the Word. And in time God gives new life through the same Word. The Word was in the beginning with God, creating, and the Word in time "became flesh and made His dwelling among us" (John 1:14). The word *life* is used to refer both to creation and to salvation in Christ. (See also Romans 4:17.)

The beginning of John's Gospel anticipates something that Jesus Himself affirms later in His ministry. In a powerful drama, the evangelist relates the story of the death of Lazarus, the brother of Jesus' friends and followers, Mary and Martha. All three were loved by Jesus. The Lord wept when He heard the news of Lazarus' death. After His remarkable declaration, "I am the resurrection and the life" (John 11:25), Jesus validated His authority and power to give life. He called Lazarus forth from the tomb and brought him through death to live again.

The story of Lazarus is, obviously, a singular miracle. We cannot expect God to raise us to live again on earth after we die. But Jesus' words to Martha are spoken to us today: "He who believes in Me will live, even though he dies; and whoever lives and believes in Me will never die." Jesus is the bringer of life to those who are spiritually dead. He is Life Incarnate. Those who live in Him by faith live in His life. Although they will go through physical death, before God they are alive. In the midst of death, life in Christ is good news indeed!

DEAD

What is the problem to which life comes as the solution? On the surface, the answer is obvious: death. Life, however, goes deeper than ordinary, everyday perceptions of death. People experience death, or the prospect of death, in many ways. For some, death is terrifying. It is the unknown beyond this life, an entrance into the abyss. People often fear what they do not know and what they cannot see. Stories of "near death" experiences—people who claim to have died and come back to life—are common, but death remains something about which no one speaks *personally*. Death is frightening because it represents a passage into the unknowable.

> For the perishable must clothe itself with the imperishable, and the mortal with immortality. When the perishable has been clothed with the imperishable, and the mortal with immortality, then the saying that is written will come true: "Death has been swallowed up in victory." "Where, O death, is your victory? Where, O death, is your sting?" The sting of death is sin, and the power of sin is the law. But thanks be to God! He gives us the victory through our Lord Jesus Christ. (1 Corinthians 15:53–57)

Death also is terrifying because it often is painful not only for those who experience it, but also for those left behind. A woman dies at the end of an illness, whether brief or prolonged. A man dies suddenly in an accident. However death comes into our life, we seem to be taken by surprise. We are seldom ready for death. We are afraid of and want nothing to do with death. The dying are shunted off to hospitals and nursing homes where they can pass their final days out of harm's way, out of mind, and most important, out of sight. Dying people confront us with our own mortality. It's not a confrontation we welcome.

Yet some people are not frightened by death. They view it as a transition into nothingness. It is simply the end. Nothing is to be expected beyond death. The natural course of all living things, whether plants or animals or human beings, concludes in an inglorious moment. It is useless to try to find meaning in death or, for that matter, in life. We are merely biological processes on a random plant in a random universe. We live, we toil, we die. That's it.

For most of us, however, death represents loss, the most painful of all experiences. Death takes away a loved one. It separates us from the people who populate our lives. Death leaves us alone. In the face of death, we are helpless. Medical advances help cure diseases and lengthen life, but death is still the end.

No matter how one views death, what is certain is that all people experience it. No one is immune. What many do not know, however, is that physical death, as frightening and painful as it may be, is only a poor image of a more profound and serious death. By nature, all people are dead before God. Our existence as mortals stands as a stark contrast to the life that God Himself is and desires to give. One of the most basic characteristics or attributes of God is that He is alive. Only God exists in Himself, apart from all else. Everything else receives its existence, its life, from Him. He is the "living God." All other "gods," who are not gods at all, are merely idols: stone, wood, metal, paper, or, more specifically, houses, cars, stocks, and bonds.

Only in the light of God's life can we fully understand our death. Our death, rooted in Adam's sin, is the common inheritance of all people born according to the course of nature. It is a contradiction to God's life. God created us to live. He breathed life—His own life—into us. But our death is our "no" to His divine gift. We rebelled. We rejected His word. We chose death. That's why our death is so serious. Is it any wonder people are afraid? Is it any wonder we find no meaning in death? No wonder people grieve so deeply. Death is terrifying! It is a meaningless contradiction! It brings us limitless sorrow!

Behind death stands a *living* God. But on our own, we know only heartache and confusion. That's what Alma was experiencing. She knew Clarence's death was a horrible contradiction and it didn't make sense. That's why she grieved.

Alive Again!

Against her experience of loss, the Gospel as life was meaningful for Alma. She had heard the Gospel before, but now she heard it in a new, personal way. She would not have to fend for herself. God was with her. Where once she thought

Clarence's death had no meaning, she came to focus on the meaning God had given to Clarence's life, and therefore to hers, through the new life He had given to both of them through faith in Jesus. She would learn to live with grief and loss. She had lost a part of herself and would not easily recover from that. Even Jesus wept at Lazarus' death, grieving the death of a loved one. He, too, felt a sense of loss. But Jesus' word was good news: life! Out of the fear, meaninglessness, and pain of death, we actually can live because Jesus, the Son of God, is the resurrection and the life.

> "For just as the Father raises the dead and gives them life, even so the Son gives life to whom He is pleased to give it. Moreover, the Father judges no one, but has entrusted all judgment to the Son, that all may honor the Son just as they honor the Father. He who does not honor the Son does not honor the Father, who sent Him. I tell you the truth, whoever hears My word and believes Him who sent Me has eternal life and will not be condemned; he has crossed over from death to life." (John 5:21–24)

At best, our lives in this present age are only a faint image of the life to come. God's promise is the rock on which we stand when our lives become especially burdensome. Death, our last enemy, has been defeated; "Where, O death, is your victory?" (1 Corinthians 15:55). Life has overcome death. Therefore, death is no longer the doorway into the unknown, much less into nothing. Rather, death is our portal into life, life eternal with Christ in heavenly bliss and happiness in the presence of Him who is life. With Christ standing at our end, we have both courage and meaning to live our present as those who have life.

> But if Christ is in you, your body is dead because of sin, yet your spirit is alive because of righteousness. And if the Spirit of Him who raised Jesus from the dead is living in you, He who raised Christ from the dead will also give life to your mortal bodies through His Spirit, who lives in you. (Romans 8:10–11)

5

Salvation

He said to her, "Daughter, your faith has healed you. Go in peace and be freed from your suffering." (Mark 5:34)

HEALTH AND HEALING

Gladys was disappointed. And her disappointment made her feel foolish—foolish for allowing her hopes to rise. She couldn't remember how many times she had tried some new treatment to find relief from her multiple sclerosis. There was nothing she wanted more than to walk away from her debilitating suffering. However, every time she tried something, it seemed she eventually felt worse.

Gladys finally had given in to her well-meaning sister-in-law. Julie was really into religion. She belonged to a church that promoted itself as bringing healing to those afflicted with chronic illnesses. In a moment of weakness, Gladys had agreed to go with Julie to a faith-healing service. "Just to check it out," Gladys muttered as she walked inside the building.

Once there, things began to change for Gladys. As the mood of excitement at the service built, Gladys felt it growing inside herself. All these people were filled with such hope and joy. Maybe Julie was right. If Jesus healed the paralyzed in Galilee, perhaps she could have a miracle too.

What a dumb idea! As a churchgoer herself, talk of Jesus wasn't foreign to Gladys, but in the days following the disappointing event, she was beginning to have deeper doubts. Perhaps she didn't have enough faith to be healed. Perhaps if her expectations had been higher. "You just don't have enough faith" echoed through her mind. Could this be true? How would she get more? How many times would she have to go through the humiliation of not being judged worthy?

As she sat at the kitchen table, Gladys thought about the words of her own pastor. Through their joint study of the Scriptures during a Bible study, he had helped Gladys to understand that the word for "healed" is often the same word used for "saved." Jesus had healed many people in His ministry, but the physical healing was always a visible sign of a deeper healing, of salvation. Jesus *saved* people. The physical healing was not most important; the spiritual healing, the salvation through faith in Christ Jesus, was more important. For reasons Gladys did not know, God had not healed her physically, but He had *healed* her—He had saved her. Gladys still had multiple sclerosis, but she was perfect and whole before God!

"Your Faith Has Healed You"

The word *salvation* is used often in the Bible to refer to restoration of health.[1] As Jesus traveled through Judea and Samaria during His earthly ministry, He often encountered the blind, the lame, and the sick. They found in the prophet from Nazareth a compassionate heart, so they came to Him in great numbers. Sometimes the word Jesus used to describe what He did for people was *salvation*.[2]

On one occasion, Jesus healed a woman with a hemorrhage (Mark 5:25–34). This woman had been subject to bleeding for 12 years. No one had been able to help her. When she came to Jesus and touched His cloak, she was healed immediately. Jesus didn't actually see the woman touch His clothing because the crowds were pressing in on Him. He did, however, know and feel that power had gone out of Him. When Jesus asked who had touched Him, the woman came forward and admitted it. Jesus blessed her with the words, "Daughter, your faith has *healed* you. Go in peace" (Mark 5:34, emphasis added).

Jesus' words could just as easily be translated, "Your faith has *saved* you." Of course, Jesus really did heal the woman. It was a true miracle. The bleeding stopped. The woman was restored to health. But Jesus did more. He also made her whole in God's eyes.[3] Jesus gave this gift freely to her, and she received it through faith. Her wholeness before God through faith is shown for the crowd to see in her actual, physical healing. Her healing was not the "main thing"; rather, the important message is that she was "saved" or "healed" before God. The visible healing was merely the public demonstration of her deeper, more profound, healing.

> Praise the LORD, O my soul; all my inmost being, praise His holy name. Praise the LORD, O my soul, and forget not all His benefits—who forgives all your sins and heals all your diseases, who redeems your life from the pit and crowns you with love and compassion, who satisfies your desires with good things so that your youth is renewed like the eagle's. (Psalm 103:1–5)

We must not diminish the importance of those wonderful events in which Jesus healed sick, miserable people of their afflictions. Nor do we deny the historical reality of the healings that Jesus did because of His great compassion. At the same time, we must not focus too narrowly on the physical healing. To do so fails to see the true significance of these and other miracles. They bear witness, more vividly than Jesus' own words, to the fact that, in the cross of Christ, God has eliminated all sickness and disease and has made us whole in His sight. While He has not promised to give each of us physical healing of our infirmities, He has given us healing in the most important way: in *His eyes*. All believers in Christ are healed or saved before God.

THE POOR, THE CRIPPLED, THE BLIND, AND THE LAME

In the parable of the great banquet (Luke 14:16–24), Jesus says that the kingdom of God is like a man preparing a banquet. This man invites many favored people, but no one comes; all make feeble excuses. Finally, the man sends his servants into the streets and alleys of the town to bring in the poor, the crippled, the blind, and the lame. These are the people who need the kind of healing our Lord has to give. They are welcomed into the kingdom.

Many people experience the Law as a problem with disease, chronic illness, or other loss of physical ability. This includes those who are beset by debilitating illnesses, such as multiple sclerosis or cancer, or those who are victims of accidents that result in the loss of mobility or sensory activity. In some cases, the affliction and its accompanying hardships become life's defining characteristics. Even more troubling than the pain and struggle of the physical problem is the psychological trauma that such conditions cause. Often people begin to think of themselves as less than complete, less than "normal," at least in respect to those who do not suffer such a fate. They may feel less than human. This lack of wholeness produces a void in their lives that is difficult to fill.

People with disease or disability are not the only ones who feel less than whole. A void also is experienced by people who, on the surface, appear to be completely normal. Many people feel a lack of wholeness, a vague but powerful sense that something is not right, not the way it should be. In our society, we see a general malaise that is made all the more painful for its lack of specificity. It is understandable when people who suffer from some specific and identifiable illness feel less than whole and seek "healing" from health professionals or charlatans. It is more difficult and more mysterious when the cause of physical and emotional disability cannot be identified.

What inner, unnamed disease causes people to flee their reality through drugs and alcohol? What condition causes young people to abuse their bodies, even to kill themselves, because of eating disorders? What hidden disability causes a man to ignore and forsake his wife and children for the sake of his career? Addictions, anorexia, obsessive work habits—all these are charlatans and fakes. They promise wholeness yet bring only despair.

We can understand these and other infirmities when we see them in the light of God's wholeness. Such infirmities are symptoms of a deeper problem, one that affects every single human being. They are outward signs that we are incomplete, unwholesome, diseased, and disabled before God. Before His perfection and completeness, we are imperfect and incomplete. We are less than fully what God made us to be. That's what Gladys sensed and what made her disease even more impossible to bear. Her dismay revealed that the multiple sclerosis was only a symptom of a much more serious condition. She was infirm before God. Her infirmity—sin—caused a deep rift between her and her Creator. She knew that her disease was merely a sign of human sinfulness and brokenness. The fact that the symptom didn't go away even after attempts at faith healing threatened her because she viewed it as a sign that she was not saved, or not fully saved, before God.

> Jesus asked, "Were not all ten cleansed? Where are the other nine? ... Then He said to him, "Rise and go; your faith has made you well." (Luke 17:17, 19)

WHOLE!

What a relief it was, therefore, for Gladys to realize that through faith in Jesus Christ she was healed, even though she still had to contend with multiple sclerosis. Through faith, she was able to see past the symptoms, past the pain and the disablement, to the perfection and wholeness of God. Through her Savior, God had given Gladys this gift through faith.

Through faith, Gladys was able to see that, on the cross, Christ not only saved her in some general, spiritual sense, not only bore her sins, but He bore her illness in His perfect body. He suffered from her sins and from her illness; He died because of them. He died from multiple sclerosis! He died from cancer and heart disease, alcoholism and anorexia. What's more, He rose victorious over them. Jesus is the Great Physician who, through His Word and sacraments, heals us of our illnesses before God. Gladys was whole! She, too, was healed—saved—in a way that transcended the immediacy of her disease. In God's eyes, she was perfect.

It is perhaps the great mystery in Christian theology that God should pronounce us whole in His sight but allow us to continue to suffer the ravages of sin in our lives. Of course, healing is no different than any other way of saying the Gospel. Yet with this metaphor, we exercise great care and sensitivity. We never take the illnesses and disabilities of people lightly. Disease and suffering do matter, and we always should be ready to do what we can to prolong life and relieve pain. Our God is a healer, and He chooses to heal through the means of medicine and proper living.

Yet we must never let anyone think that there is a direct, causal link between physical and spiritual health. We may never know, this side of heaven, why God allows His beloved children to suffer. Yet when we suffer, we can fervently and with much comfort proclaim that through faith in Jesus Christ we are in perfect health before God.

In this age, we walk by faith and not by sight (2 Corinthians 5:7). By sight we see suffering and illness, but by faith we see perfect wellness. Until our Lord returns, we will continue to suffer. But we can thank God that through the eyes of faith we can see through our suffering to that day when He will bring us to Himself in heaven and make us whole physically, even as He has made us whole spiritually through the gift of faith in Jesus.

ENDNOTES

1. For examples, see 2 Kings 20 and Isaiah 38:20.
2. Jesus does not always call "healing" *salvation*. At times, *forgiveness* is connected to healing, for example, see Matthew 9:2.
3. This is perhaps brought out most clearly in the account of the ten lepers (Luke 17:11–19). The lepers are not only "healed" of their illness, they are made "clean." According to Old Testament law, they were required to present themselves to the priests for verification of healing. This requirement indicates that leprosy was a form of uncleanness before God. By going to the priests, these lepers were displaying not only their healing, but their cleansing in God's eyes.

6

Light

When Jesus spoke again to the people, He said, "I am the light of the world. Whoever follows Me will never walk in darkness, but will have the light of life." (John 8:12)

LIGHT SHINING IN DARKNESS

Jason was confused. He thought life should have begun to make sense by the time he was a junior at the university. But it hadn't. In fact, he was more confused than ever. The more he learned, the less he knew.

Now in his course on the postmodern worldview, the situation had grown worse. Jason was learning that many contemporary philosophers and linguists were making a compelling case that there is no unified field theory, no universal truth, no knowledge that can help a person make sense of life. Jason wondered what would become of his search for meaning. Was it all in vain? Why was he going to school? He seemed to be in the dark.

Jason asked his parents for guidance, but they were not much help. His pastor didn't know much about postmodernism either. Finally, almost in desperation, Jason went to see his advisor, Professor Luz, who taught philosophy at the university. She helped Jason to see that while the human perspective is important, life is more than "what you see is what you get." In addition to the phenomena that surround us, which we can see and measure and quantify, there is a deeper, or higher, reality that gives meaning to what we experience. Philosophers call this the metaphysical. Theologians call it God. For Christians, God, especially as He has revealed Himself in Christ, enables us to make sense of our reality. Jason was elated. This is what he had always thought, but Professor Luz brought clarity to his vague understanding.

We need light from above to understand the world. God enlightens our darkened minds so we may know the truth.

"I Am the Light of the World"

Light is one of the most "illuminating" metaphors, common to both the Old and New Testaments. The *light* metaphor does double—even triple—duty. First, light indicates wisdom or knowledge of the truth as opposed to ignorance or falsehood or error. Second, light evokes goodness as opposed to evil, which always seems to lurk in the darkness. Finally, light stands for life as opposed to the darkness where no one can survive for long. *Light* is an extremely rich and complex metaphor. In fact, perhaps it would be better to refer to *metaphors* because each use of light has its own sphere or semantic field. All three metaphors referred to by the single word *light* are found abundantly in Scripture.

A primary text in the gospels that deals with light is John 1:1–18, a text also used in the discussion of the *life* metaphor. The development of the *light* metaphor in John's prologue gives an indication of its importance for the rest of the Gospel.

> In Him was life, and that life was the light of men. The light shines in the darkness, but the darkness has not understood it. There came a man who was sent from God; his name was John. He came as a witness to testify concerning that light, so that through him all men might believe. He himself was not the light; he

came only as a witness to the light. The true light that gives light to every man was coming into the world. (John 1:4–9)

The central feature of God's saving activity in the world is spoken of as "the light [that] shines in the darkness" (John 1:5). This world—shrouded in death, evil, and ignorance—cannot overcome the light.[1] Darkness is painted with the hues of evil and opposition to God's plan of salvation. Darkness, as evil, tries to overcome the light. John makes it clear, however, that those who believe in the light do so because of the will of God, not because of their own decision. The scope of the light's shining is universal. It is the cause of the believers' calling and identity as children of God.

We have "seen His glory, the glory of the One and Only, who came from the Father, full of grace and truth" (John 1:14). This light enabled John and the other apostles to see the only begotten Son of the Father. Light gives vision to see who Christ truly is. He Himself later testifies, "I am the light of the world" (John 8:12). In other words, light enables one to see the grace and truth of God. John brings this out more clearly when he writes: "No one has ever seen God, but God the One and Only [that is, the only begotten of God], who is at the Father's side, has made Him known" (John 1:18). The Light, who is Christ, enables us to see, to know, God. He shows the way to God by His light.

Jesus affirms John's testimony concerning the light when He says in John 8:12, "I am the light of the world." But notice the language: Jesus *is* the light. He is light incarnate, light personified. He is the one who came into this world darkened by death, evil, and ignorance. In His light, in Him *as* light, we are able to see the meaning of all things.

LIVING (OR DYING) IN THE DARK

In light of this metaphor, how do we experience the Law? First, we recognize death and deprivation. Light is necessary for life as we know it. Darkness is the absence of light, the absence of light's life-giving qualities. Darkness is being deprived of what is necessary for survival. What happens when plants do not receive enough light? They suffer, perhaps die. What happens when humans are deprived of light? They, too, can suffer serious physical and psychological damage. Also darkness often is cold, a further detriment to life. In short, darkness is a metaphor for death.

People experience the Law as death, perceiving it through the lens of darkness. They feel as though their lives are being "snuffed out" or slowly smothered. They feel deprived of something necessary to continue living. As relationships "grow cold," people are "left out in the cold." They lack life-giving warmth and are barely able to keep the flame of life aglow. This deprivation is a slow but certain death. It is a certain death because in the darkness we are deprived of something we absolutely need for survival.

> "Arise, shine, for your light has come, and the glory of the Lord rises upon you. See, darkness covers the earth and thick darkness is over the peoples, but the Lord rises upon you and His glory appears over you. Nations will come to your light, and kings to the brightness of your dawn. (Isaiah 60:1–3)

EVIL

Another key facet to the *light* metaphor is the concept of darkness as evil. Few things elicit greater fear in people than darkness. Although most of us grew out of our childish fear of monsters under the bed and in the closet, which accompanied our fear of the darkness, we retain our fear of the dark itself. As children, we simply asked someone to turn on the hall light or to give us a night-light. Now our fears are greater. Who would go into a dark alley at night? How many people are afraid of caves and other dark places? Darkness instills fear in us, even as adults, because darkness is the abode of evil.

Evil flourishes in dark places—in back streets and alleys, behind closed doors, in hidden places. It is under the cover of darkness that people do evil deeds. A testimony to the power of this metaphor is that the open commission of an evil deed is considered to be worse because it is done "in broad daylight." Many people live their lives in terror of the evil that lies around the next corner. Some are even afraid to leave their own homes.

More frightening still to some people is the evil that lurks in the darkness of their own hearts. They fear the truth will be brought to light. They do not want their sins exposed for the world to see. Perhaps this is because they love their sins and don't want to give them up. If they can "keep things under wraps," perhaps they will be able to continue uninterrupted in their sins. As long as it's "under the cover of darkness," we feel secure in our sinful actions. The *darkness* metaphor reveals more than the evil "out there"; it reveals the evil within each sinful heart.

Darkness as Ignorance

Darkness is also a potent metaphor for ignorance. We commonly speak of ourselves as being "in the dark" when we lack knowledge. People experience their problem in life as not knowing the way, lacking specific knowledge that would help everything make sense. A major malady today is a lack of meaning for life. In this Information Age, people are on a quest for knowledge from every conceivable source: New Age enlightenment, self-help wisdom, and science and technology. Name it, produce it, and people will buy it. They hope to fill a void in their lives with some sort of knowledge. If we only could learn the right way, discover the key to understanding, develop the power of positive thinking, everything would be clear.

Because we are ignorant, we are lost. We do not know the way. We stumble and grope in the darkness. We wander into unsafe places because we cannot see where we are going. The path is hidden from our sight. We are hopeless to find our way; we are confused, blind, and benighted.

Identifying our problem as darkness helps us appreciate the seriousness of our sinfulness before God. The reason so many people experience existence as deprivation is because they *are* deprived not of some vague generalities, but of the very substance of life. Darkness involves shielding ourselves from the source of light and life. Of course we *feel* dead; we *are* dead. In this void, we only can shrivel and die. But our sin involves us in a problem far more serious.

We are evil. That's what the Bible says. It's not only criminals in dark streets who are evil. There is more than enough evil in our sinful hearts. We try, in vain, to shield our evil deeds from the light of God's Word. But the light of His Law penetrates our most secret sins.

We are theologically ignorant. Jason needed to learn that his problem was not just that he lacked wisdom or knowledge. It wasn't the acquisition of knowledge *per se* that would bring enlightenment, but it is the knowledge of the one who is Light that brings enlightenment. All the wisdom in the world would not help Jason make sense of reality. Something absolutely necessary was missing from his search. Without that foundation, he was doomed to search blindly all his life.

The Light that Enlightens Every Man

When compared to how we blindly search for meaning, hearing the Gospel as *light* is good news. It says that God has revealed—He has provided—what we need to survive. He revives us with the warmth of His light and brings us back to life. He chases away the evil of this dark world with His light and enables us to live safely in the light of His love. He shows us the way to true knowledge, to the knowledge of the Truth, so we need not continue to stumble and fall.

> The God of this age has blinded the minds of unbelievers, so that they cannot see the light of the gospel of the glory of Christ, who is the image of God. For we do not preach ourselves, but Jesus Christ as Lord, and ourselves as your servants for Jesus' sake. For God, who said, "Let light shine out of darkness," made His light shine in our hearts to give

us the light of the knowledge of the glory of God in the face
of Christ. (2 Corinthians 4:4–6)

Jason's frantic search for meaning is over. So is ours. Our
attempt to make sense of life finds its completion in Christ,
the Light of the world. He is "the way and the truth and the
life" (John 14:6). If we have seen Jesus, we have seen God. The
search is over. It ends not as we ascend a sacred mountain to
commune with the gods and receive special wisdom, but as
God descends to us in the person of Jesus Christ. Here, in this
darkened world, He shines His light. Here, into our darkened
hearts, He gives the light of His grace and favor.

God gave His light to us not by taking us out of the darkness, but by entering into our darkness, by being enveloped in
the darkness of our death, by being oppressed by the darkness
of our evil, by experiencing the darkness of our ignorance.
"From the sixth hour until the ninth hour darkness came over
all the land," Matthew records in his Gospel (Matthew 27:45).
On the cross, Jesus went into the darkness. He became the
"darkness of the world" for us so we might be the "light of the
world" (Matthew 5:14).

We no longer live in the darkness. We bask in the light,
in the life, in the goodness and wisdom of Christ's light. In this
age, the darkness always lurks nearby, seeking to envelope us
once again. In this age, we live as "children of light" (Ephesians
5:8) in a world still groping in darkness. But having seen the
Light, we know the Way. We know that our end is in that city
where "[t]hey will not need the light of a lamp or the light of the
sun, for the Lord God will give them light" (Revelation 22:5).

ENDNOTE

1. The Greek word translated as *overcome* (New International Version footnote, also in the New Revised Standard Version) is,
in fact, difficult to translate. Some experts render the word as
understand or *comprehend* (see the New American Standard Bible).
The translation "snuff it out" is intriguing because it is evocative
of extinguishing a candle or lamp. In John's Gospel, the light
meets with opposition from the darkness.

LIGHT

7

Bread and Water

"I am the bread of life. He who comes to Me will never go hungry, and he who believes in Me will never be thirsty." (John 6:35)

HUNGRY AND THIRSTY

After 26 years in a good marriage and after raising three children to adulthood and self-sufficiency, Penelope couldn't explain the sense of emptiness she was feeling. She had a fruitful life and could think of nothing specific that she lacked. She and her husband, Roger, had done quite well and were living comfortably. Still Penelope had a vague, undefined sense of dissatisfaction. She craved something more, but she couldn't put her finger on what it was.

One day Penelope succumbed to her friend Gloria's weekly invitation to attend a women's Bible study. She always had avoided attending because religious people made her feel uncomfortable. But Penelope went, mostly to get Gloria off her back.

The women were studying Jesus' Sermon on the Mount, going verse by verse through the Beatitudes. Someone read, "Blessed are those who hunger and thirst for righteousness, for they will be filled" (Matthew 5:6). Penelope was startled. Is that what her problem was? Is that why she felt so empty, even though on the surface her life was full? Was she hungering and thirsting after righteousness? Would that fill her?

BREAD OF LIFE AND LIVING WATER

Among the more visceral metaphors for the Gospel are
those that refer to eating or drinking the blessings of Christ.
The primary way of saying this is to use the most common elements in the biblical world: bread and water. Of course, these
are still among the most common elements today, so their
power as metaphor is still strong. Although eating and drinking are different from each other, they belong together because
they both evoke a way of understanding our reception of the
Gospel: We receive by the mouth.

Both of these ways of saying the Gospel—eating or drinking God's gifts in faith—are common in the Old Testament
too. Eating was an important means of fellowship in ancient
times. Partaking of numerous meals together is richly suggestive of the bonds that exist between people. Likewise, *water*
and *drinking* as a metaphor for receiving the blessings of God
is common in the Old Testament. The New Testament inherits
and builds on both metaphors.

In John 6, Jesus is teaching the multitudes of people on
the far shore of the Sea of Galilee. Jesus multiplied the five
barley loaves and two fish to feed the 5,000 men gathered
there. When they were finished eating their fill, 12 baskets of
leftovers were gathered. The feeding of the 5,000 became the
background for a sermon that Jesus preached the next day.
When some asked Him about the manna that came down
from heaven during the desert wanderings of the Israelites,
Jesus said:

> "I tell you the truth, it is not Moses who has given you
> the bread from heaven, but it is My Father who gives
> you the true bread from heaven. For the bread of God is
> He who comes down from heaven and gives life to the
> world. ... I am the bread of life. He who comes to Me

will never go hungry, and he who believes in Me will never be thirsty." (John 6:32–33, 35)

In this passage, another of the great "I am" statements of Jesus in John's Gospel,[1] Jesus makes the remarkable claim that He is bread—not just any bread, but the bread of God that comes down from heaven. Moreover, Jesus is the bread that gives life to the world in such a way that those who eat it will never hunger again. To receive Jesus by faith means to receive sustenance for life, to receive nourishment for our souls. We are satisfied, satiated, with what is really necessary for life. We are filled with good food, food from heaven.

The Gospel of John also develops the *water* metaphor. In John 4:4–26, the account of Jesus' encounter with the Samaritan woman at the well of Sychar, Jesus is sitting by the well when a woman comes to draw water. He asks her for a drink of water. He then says, "Everyone who drinks this water will be thirsty again, but whoever drinks the water I give him will never thirst. Indeed, the water I give him will become in him a spring of water welling up to eternal life" (John 4:13–14).

Here Jesus does not actually say, as He did in the case of the bread, that He is the water. But He does promise that He will give the water of life. The metaphor is softer yet still vivid.[2] If a person drinks the water Jesus gives—if a person believes in Jesus—he or she will never thirst again. Jesus quenches thirst in a way that lasts forever. In fact, He gives to the recipient an internal spring of water for eternity—water that is fully and eternally satisfying.

Parched and Hungry

Everyone knows what it is like to be hungry and thirsty. That's the beauty of this metaphor: It is universally understood. But many people in the world are *always* hungry. They are literally starving. They experience the Law as hunger in a direct and immediate way. Famine is a pervasive threat to millions. How tragic and painful it is when people do not get enough food and fall victim to malnourishment. Although starvation affects all ages, it is especially difficult to watch infants, small children, and the elderly suffer.

> "Come, all you who are thirsty, come to the waters; and you who have no money, come, buy and eat! Come, buy wine and milk without money and without cost. Why spend money on what is not bread, and your labor on what does not satisfy? Listen, listen to Me, and eat what is good, and your soul will delight in the richest of fare. Give ear and come to Me; hear Me, that your soul may live. I will make an everlasting covenant with you, My faithful love promised to David. (Isaiah 55:1–3)

Likewise, we have a sense of what it is like to suffer from extreme thirst. Although we never may have experienced it directly, we have seen or read about those who die of dehydration. For those who inhabit inhospitable areas where water is scarce, this resource is infinitely precious. The tragic consequences of running out of water are well known.

Millions of people have a less immediate hunger and thirst, but one that is no less harmful. Famine and drought are common today, even in areas where there is plenty to eat and drink. People feel a void, an emptiness, an undefined and general dissatisfaction. Although their lives are filled with good, they sense something is lacking. They are hungry and thirsty spiritually. Many are starving and parched, even amid plenty. In their search for satisfaction, people stuff themselves with a steady diet of spiritual junk food. Sects and cults never have been more popular. We see an unparalleled demand for spiritual gurus and advisors. People are gorging themselves on food with no nutritional value and guzzling drink that does not quench thirst. They are overweight from eating, yet they are dying from malnutrition. They have drunk every last drop, yet they are dying from dehydration. They are eating spoiled food and drinking deadly poison, consuming food and drink that kills.

This is, in a way, what Penelope was sensing in her life. She realized that her hunger and thirst were much deeper than she originally thought. She was hungry and thirsty because she was eating the wrong food and drinking the wrong water. Cut off from God, the true source of life, she could eat only imitation food that did not satisfy because it could not. Continuing to live without faith in Christ meant a slow, agonizing death.

SATISFIED!

Because of this sense of something lacking, Penelope heard the Beatitude "Blessed are those who hunger and thirst for righteousness, for they will be filled" as good news. What is truly filling, truly satisfying, is the righteousness of Christ. He is the Bread of life. He gives the water of life. He fills us abundantly with a never-ending banquet of fine food and drink. He provides us with a table that overflows with edible, nourishing food. When we partake of Christ through faith, we will not be disappointed. Christ will satisfy us by giving us what we really need: the Bread of God.

The Lord's Supper, too, is a wonderful gift from Christ. Our Lord nourishes us with His body and blood, which we eat and drink for the forgiveness of our sins. Clearly, our eating and drinking is not only spiritual, but also actual. By faith we eat and drink forgiveness while by our mouths we eat and drink the body and blood of Christ with the bread and the wine. In this precious Meal, our Lord invites us to eat and drink and be satisfied.

In this life, there always will be vestiges of hunger and thirst. Our craving for unhealthy food never will be wholly put away. Yet as we hunger and thirst after righteousness, as we eat and drink and are satisfied with the wholesome bread and water of Christ, we are reminded of that day when we will sit at the banquet table with our Lord in heaven and eat and drink with Him forever.

> For I received from the Lord what I also passed on to you: The Lord Jesus, on the night He was betrayed, took bread, and when He had given thanks, He broke it and said, "This is My body, which is for you; do this in remembrance of Me."

In the same way, after supper He took the cup, saying, "This cup is the new covenant in My blood; do this, whenever you drink it, in remembrance of Me." For whenever you eat this bread and drink this cup, you proclaim the Lord's death until He comes. (1 Corinthians 11:23–26)

ENDNOTES

1. John's Gospel contains eight sayings of Jesus in which He predicates of Himself divine prerogatives: "I am the bread of life" (6:35, 41, 48, 51); "I am the light of the world" (8:12; 9:5); "I am the gate for the sheep" (10:7, 9); "I am the good shepherd" (10:11, 14); "I am the resurrection and the life" (11:25); "I am the way and the truth and the life" (14:6); "I am the true vine" (15:1, 5); and "before Abraham was born, I am" (8:58). This last saying is unique in that Jesus speaks of His pre-existence. The significance of these sayings is that they are suggestive of the Hebrew name of God, Yahweh, which can be translated "I am." Thus, Jesus may be heard to be appropriating to Himself the divine name (Exodus 3:14).

2. As the story in John 6 progresses, Jesus gets more clear as His hearers get more antagonistic. Finally, in verse 53, Jesus says, "I tell you the truth, unless you eat the flesh of the Son of Man and drink His blood, you have no life in you." He goes on to speak in terms that are highly suggestive of the Lord's Supper. We cannot here enter into the debate as to whether this passage is in any way eucharistic. However, it is clear that Christians often have heard an echo of Christ's later words spoken on the night when He was betrayed and often have made the connection. It is, indeed, tempting to connect the eating of the Bread of life by faith and the eating of the bread in the Lord's Supper.

JUST WORDS

PART 3

CHRIST THE REDEEMER: COMMERCE METAPHORS

8

Ransom

For you know that it was not with perishable things such as silver or gold that you were redeemed from the empty way of life handed down to you from your fore-fathers, but with the precious blood of Christ, a lamb without blemish or defect. (1 Peter 1:18–19)

NOT WITH PERISHABLE THINGS

Richard felt as though he were on a treadmill, and he didn't know how to get off. This wasn't what he had in mind when he got his master's degree in business. To all appearances, he was successful: a beautiful home filled with the best possessions, an imported car with all the gadgets, the most expensive clothes, a lovely wife, and two beautiful children. He had it all. He was on top of the world, or so it seemed. But that was a thin veneer.

Inside, Richard felt imprisoned. He was burdened by bills he couldn't keep up with—a mortgage, car payments, private school tuition, the whole nine yards. These commitments kept him in a job he didn't like and didn't find rewarding because he needed it to maintain his lifestyle. Richard was in the prison of his own riches, and it was beginning to show in his relationships and in his job performance. He would give anything, pay any price, to be free of these burdens. But he knew money couldn't buy freedom. In fact, he was finding out that money can cause slavery.

One day at work, Richard confided his feelings to his friend Derrick. Derrick immediately understood and told Richard that he had once felt the same way. When asked to explain how he had overcome his slavery to money, Derrick told Richard that he had discovered riches greater and more lasting than money and possessions. Derrick told Richard that, through faith in Jesus, he had discovered that the greatest riches are those you can't earn. Rather, the greatest riches are those that simply are given to you.

Richard started thinking about all this. Perhaps he had been guilty of thinking that the only wealth that counted was measured in terms of material possessions. Perhaps there were other treasures that were more important. Derrick certainly seemed to be happy. Maybe he ought to look into this thing called faith and see if the possession of some imperishable riches might help him feel less imprisoned and hemmed in by his life.

A Ransom for Many

The commerce or transaction metaphors in Scripture are among the most vivid and helpful ways to proclaim the Gospel. These metaphors use language and imagery that is universally understood. You don't need a business degree to understand the concept of barter and exchange. Everyone knows the idea of offering one thing in trade for another, whether it be in-kind services or shells or precious metals or paper money.

Although most people aren't aware of it, some of the most popular Gospel language in the Bible comes from the realm of commerce. The language of the marketplace is borrowed to convey the implications of Christ's suffering and death on the cross. Jesus Himself chose to speak of His work in this way—in the language of ransom.

In Matthew 20:28, Jesus characterizes His entire work and ministry: "The Son of Man did not come to be served, but to serve, and to give His life as a ransom for many." *Ransom* is a word that evokes the marketplace, particularly the slave market.[1] The ransom was the price paid to purchase a servant or slave from indenture or slavery. In this passage, Jesus says that He came to be a servant, not to be served.[2] Jesus is playing all the roles. He is the servant—perhaps it would be better to say *slave*—standing in our place. He is the one who came to pay the price for securing the freedom of those in slavery. And He is the price paid, the ransom required to secure the slaves' freedom.[3] Christ is everything in this transaction.

The *ransom* metaphor pictures those whom Jesus came to purchase as helpless slaves, chained in the marketplace, standing on the auction block with no hope of freedom. For all they know, they will be purchased by an evil taskmaster as bad as the one in whose chains they now stand. Amazingly, along comes Jesus. He takes His place among the slaves, fully identifying with them, becoming one of them. Then He pays the price for their freedom, and, incredibly, the price is His own life. His precious blood (Hebrews 9:12) is poured out on the auction block of the cross. The image is powerful.

POWERLESS SLAVES

We've already seen hints at how the Law is experienced in light of the *ransom* metaphor. Of course, many people do live as slaves, indentured servants in the grip of taskmasters who exploit them for as much profit as they can get. Often the greatest victims are the young and the elderly, who are especially susceptible to the hardships of slavery and may not have the protection of earthly legal systems. People in bondage know directly and immediately the full force of the Law's crushing slavery.

Others know about slavery less directly, but no less forcefully. Because they lack financial resources or access to education, many people are held as slaves to an oppressive reality. Stuck in the urban jungle, assaulted by crime and violence at every turn, living in the mean streets of the inner city, plagued by poor services and decaying schools, many live a life of virtual captivity. They feel imprisoned, even though no physical barricade surrounds them. They have no hope of getting out, no hope of making their lives better. They are poverty's slaves locked in a jail of bricks and concrete.

But the *ransom* metaphor also speaks powerfully to those who live in unparalleled affluence and appear proud of their accomplishments, certain that their wealth and freedom is a sign of favorable standing before God. In more wealthy and developed parts of the world, bondage and captivity are experienced in another way. Many people feel trapped in the pursuit of possessions. They feel compelled to continue to accumulate things in an effort to "keep up with the Joneses." They think that the gathering of goods will give them freedom, but it seldom does. The freedom is fleeting, and when it leaves, they are all the more helpless and hopeless about finding a way out of the prison. The walls that hold them captive are not physical, but they are just as real.

What people need to know is that the bondage they feel is symptomatic of a much deeper and more vexing slavery, one that affects all humankind. We are, in addition to our other enslavements, theological slaves. We are captives before God.

Our real problem is that we are spiritual slaves, held in the strong chains of an evil taskmaster. In fact, we commonly speak of a threefold master who holds us captive: the devil, the world, and our sinful flesh. Satan is an oppressive slave driver, driving us further from our God. The world would draw us deeper into slavery, enticing us with its fleeting and perishable goods. Our sinful flesh, perhaps the most oppressive master of all, constantly tempts us to lust after those things that cannot satisfy and that soon perish. We are held tightly in the strong chains of these masters. Without someone to purchase our freedom, we certainly will die in our slavery.

For there is one God and one mediator between God and men, the man Christ Jesus, who gave Himself as a ransom for all men—the testimony given in its proper time. (1 Timothy 2:5–6)

Free!

Richard may not have been able to articulate it, but his sense of captivity to the things of his life was really only a window into his real situation before God: his slavery to sin and death. Once he realized this, Richard could begin to grasp the magnitude of what God had done for him in sending His only Son, Jesus Christ, to be the payment to buy back the freedom of the world.

Imagine it! There you are, on the slave block, about to be sold into who knows what kind of slavery. You look up, and there stands Jesus, giving Himself for you, standing in your chains, shedding His blood for you, buying your freedom. "You are free to go," you hear the auctioneer say. "You are free!" The price? The eternally valuable blood of Jesus Christ, the priceless perfection of His obedience in life and in death, the precious treasury of His merit on the cross. This was the payment to buy freedom for the entire world.

To whom did Jesus pay the ransom?[4] In one sense, He paid the price demanded from the Father. There always will be a *theological* dimension to Christ's work. What happened at the cross was the satisfaction of God's demands; Christ dealt with our problem with God. Of course, God is not the evil taskmaster from whom we needed to be freed. Nor was the ransom paid to Satan. Although a worthy foe, Satan never had such a great role to play in our redemption that he could demand or receive anything from God. Christ is all in all—the slave, the ransom, and the purchaser.

The price has been fully paid. No price was too great for God to buy back His beloved people. With God nothing is impossible. Christ has accomplished the greatest task of all: He has bought us back from the evil taskmasters who oppressed us. We no longer are subject to the devil, the world, and our sinful flesh. We have been freed. Our chains have been loosed.

Ransom through Christ also has a strong eschatological emphasis. Our ransom is connected with Christ's return. In Ephesians 4:30, Paul speaks of the "Holy Spirit of God, with whom you were sealed for the *day of redemption*" (emphasis added). This is a reminder that the freedom God gives us through faith in Christ is not necessarily physical and material. When Christians are freed from oppressive situations, they naturally will attribute it to God's providential care and give Him all the glory. On the other hand, we also know that the liberation God gives us is theological liberation, freedom from the enslaving effects of sin. We do not expect that God always will free us from our physical or material bondage. Instead, we await the day of our redemption when we will see by sight the freedom we now see only by faith.

> We wait for the blessed hope—the glorious appearing of our great God and Savior, Jesus Christ, who gave Himself for us to redeem us from all wickedness and to purify for Himself a people that are His very own, eager to do what is good. (Titus 2:13–14)

ENDNOTES

1. The Greek word translated as "ransom" is *apolytrosis*. Although related to the word *redeem,* the word *ransom* has its own nuances.
2. The Greek word translated as "servant," *diakonos,* is the origin of the English word *deacon.*
3. The text says that Jesus came to give His life as a ransom "for many." This, however, should not be understood to mean that Jesus was a ransom only for some and not for others. Rather, as a common biblical usage, "many" often can have the force of "all." Besides, while Jesus came to ransom all, not all will be set free because this gift is to be received through faith. For more information, see 1 Timothy 2:6, which, in its echoes of Jesus' words in Matthew 20:28, says, "who gave Himself as a ransom for all men."
4. A lot of mischief has been done in relation to commercial metaphors. The so-called "dramatic" theory of the atonement sug-

gested that God paid Satan to set his captives free. See Harold
O. J. Brown, *Heresies: The Image of Christ in the Mirror of Heresy
and Orthodoxy from the Apostles to the Present* (Garden City, N.Y.:
Doubleday, 1994).

9

Redemption

Do you not know that your body is a temple of the Holy Spirit, who is in you, whom you have received from God? You are not your own; you were brought at a price. Therefore honor God with your body. (1 Corinthians 6:19–20)

MASTERS OF OUR OWN DESTINY

Bob was a self-made man. That's the way he had been brought up. He had been taught that the greatest good was to be free. So he was self-sufficient and self-reliant. He held to the motto he had learned in his childhood: "If you want something done right, do it yourself." That's the way he had built his successful trucking business—with hard work, sacrifice, and a "never count on anyone else to do what you can do" attitude. No charity, no handouts. Take what's coming to you and make the best of what you've got. That was Bob's philosophy. It gave him independence and freedom. It made him the master of his destiny.

As Bob sat in church one Sunday morning, his pastor referred to a passage that sounded strange. The pastor quoted from 1 Corinthians 6:19–20: "You are not your own; you were bought at a price." At first Bob was offended. It contradicted everything he had understood to be true about himself.

Bob stewed on this passage for the rest of the day and for much of the rest of the week. He felt as though his independence were threatened. Finally, Bob talked with his pastor, who helped Bob see that the apostle's words didn't take away freedom and independence at all. Rather, they made possible the greatest freedom imaginable. When we live in Christ through faith, we are the most free we can be. When we are not our own, but God's, we are most truly ourselves. When we are not masters of our own destiny, but our destinies are mastered by God, we are truly free.

Bought at a Price

The idea that Christ has purchased us or redeemed us is closely related to the *ransom* metaphor. Redemption also comes out of the background of the slave market. While the *ransom* metaphor focuses on the *price* that is paid, the *redemption* metaphor focuses on the *act* of paying the price. God redeems us; now redeemed, we are owned by God. These two ideas—ransom and redemption—are nearly inseparable, but they do look at Christ's work from different perspectives.

Redemption hardly seems like a metaphor. It's so common in our Gospel vocabulary that we often use it without even thinking of its commercial background. *Redemption* is, unfortunately, a "dead" Gospel metaphor. Yet in its evocation of the slave market and the idea of transaction, it is a richly textured word, one that is prominent in the Old Testament, especially in many messianic prophecies that point forward to Jesus.

> Why have You rejected us forever, O God? Why does Your anger smolder against the sheep of Your pasture? Remember the people You purchased of old, the tribe of Your inheritance, whom You redeemed—Mount Zion, where You dwelt. (Psalm 74:1–2)

One of the fullest uses of the *redemption* metaphor is found in Paul's letter to the Galatians. Although Paul uses a variety of metaphors to speak the Gospel in this epistle, including *adoption* and *inheritance,* he refers powerfully to *redemption.* Paul writes: "Christ redeemed us from the curse of the Law by becoming a curse for us, for it is written, 'Cursed is everyone who is hung on a tree' " (Galatians 3:13).[1] Our redemption in Christ is like a transaction: The curse we deserved for having defiled the Holy Land through our sin is transferred to Christ. He makes the payment. He takes our place beneath the curse of God. A great exchange takes place, whereby our curse becomes His and His blessing becomes ours.

Later in Galatians, Paul refers again to the redemption of those imprisoned under the Law: "But when the time had fully come, God sent His Son, born of a woman, born under Law, to redeem those under Law, that we might receive the full rights of sons" (Galatians 4:4–5). This time Paul refers to the central feature of God's redemption of the world—the sending of His Son into the world to buy back those under the Law. Jesus came to purchase us back. Notice also the great exchange: The Son of God is born under the Law in our place so we, who by nature were not the children of God, might receive the full rights of sons. By a great exchange, a purchase, a redemption, Christ has made us His own.

MASTERED

In light of the *redemption* metaphor, how is the Law experienced? It certainly does damage to our self-image. Although we like to think of ourselves as self-sufficient, we are not. Although we like to think of ourselves as free and independent, we are not. Although we like to think of ourselves as masters of our own destiny, we are not. We are insufficient, bound, and dependent. We are mastered by forces beyond our control. What makes our situation worse is the illusion that we are truly independent. *How pitiful, we muse, for an indentured servant to think he is free or for a slave to think he is the master.* But we are not in charge. Our plight is this: We imagine we are in charge.

We are chattel. We are owned lock, stock, and barrel, but we are convinced we are free. Nothing we could do or say, nothing we could pay, could buy our independence. Our dire situation is only worsened by the delusion that we are free. Our independence is a ruse, our self-sufficiency a charade, our mastery of destiny a lie.

Why? Because before God we are bound in our sins and trespasses. We have no freedom to better ourselves in God's eyes, no sufficiency to move Him to favor us with His grace. We are held fast in the chains of our sin, bound in our slavery to our evil inclination, under the curse of God's Law, and without the rights of God's free children. No matter what we think, we cannot buy our way out of this slavery. We may fool ourselves into thinking we are masters, but the Master is not fooled. That's what Bob recognized about himself. He realized that he was not the master of his own fate. Rather, before God, Bob was enslaved. Once he came to see this truth, Bob was ready to hear about true freedom.

> Christ redeemed us from the curse of the Law by becoming a curse for us, for it is written: "Cursed is everyone who is hung on a tree." He redeemed us in order that the blessing given to Abraham might come to the Gentiles through Christ Jesus, so that by faith we might receive the promise of the Spirit. (Galatians 3:13–14)

THE GREAT EXCHANGE

Christ has exchanged our slavery for freedom, our insufficiency for sufficiency. He did this, amazingly, as He took His place among the slaves as *one* of the slaves. He was a willing slave, Paul says. Christ "made Himself nothing, taking the very nature of a servant" (Philippians 2:7).[2] He was a slave not because He had to be (like us!), but because He chose to be (for us!). In His living, Christ bound Himself to a life of obedience and service. In His dying, He "chained" Himself to the "slave market" of the cross where He died the death of a slave. As a result, we are free.

90

What a wonderful exchange! Our Lord exchanged places with us. He became a curse so we might be blessed. He was born under the Law so we might have the full rights of children. He became a slave so we might become free. He died so we might live. He purchased our freedom. He, the slave, became our Master. What a beautiful message: "We are not our own, we have been bought at a price"!

Paul continues: "Therefore honor God with your body" (1 Corinthians 6:20). Even those who have faith in Christ are not absolutely free to do anything they wish. We could never handle absolute freedom. The idea that we can handle freedom is a sinful delusion. What Christ has done is to bring us back from our previous evil owners so we might be owned again by our proper Master—God. Jesus restored us to our loving Father as our Master; we are now willing and blessed "slaves" of God. In a paradoxical way, therefore, the Christian is, as Martin Luther wrote, both bound to no one and servant of all.[3] We are free from the coercion of the Law, and, like the one in whom we live by faith, we freely subject ourselves to God and to one another. In other words, giving up mastery of our destiny, we joyfully become "mastered by destiny."

ENDNOTES

1. Paul connects Deuteronomy 21:23 with the cross of Jesus, metaphorically referring to the "cross" as a "tree."
2. The Greek word translated in the NIV as "servant" here means "slave."
3. Martin Luther, "The Freedom of the Christian," in *Career of the Reformer I*, vol. 31 of *Luther's Works* (Philadelphia: Fortress Press, 1957).

10

Property

In Him we have redemption through His blood, the forgiveness of sins, in accordance with the riches of God's grace ... . And you also were included in Christ when you heard the word of truth, the Gospel of your salvation. Having believed, you were marked in Him with a seal, the promised Holy Spirit, who is a deposit guaranteeing our inheritance until the redemption of those who are God's possession—to the praise of His glory. (Ephesians 1:7, 13–14)

THE RICHES OF GOD'S GRACE

Cheryl was at her wit's end. She simply didn't know where to turn. Her welfare check lasted only about half the month. Although she wanted to, and had tried several times, she was unable to work because there was no one to watch her two children and daycare was too expensive. She lived in a run-down apartment in a small town with little opportunity for a change in her situation. She wanted her children to have more opportunities than she had, but she just couldn't make ends meet. Instead, she fell farther behind every month. She felt trapped.

Cheryl liked to attend the women's Bible study that met weekly at the church down the street. There was free baby-sitting, which gave her a chance to talk to adults and to get a break from the kids.

One day, the leader read from Ephesians 1. Several verses stuck in Cheryl's mind: "In Him we have redemption through His blood, the forgiveness of sins, in accordance with the riches of God's grace ... you were marked in Him with a seal ... until the redemption of those who are God's possession" (Ephesians 1:7, 14). The words *riches* and *possession* struck her as odd. She wondered what it meant to have riches even though she was poor. What could it mean to have possessions even though she had nothing to call her own?

After the study, Cheryl talked with Mrs. Carson, the Bible study leader. Mrs. Carson told Cheryl that though she was poor in material things, she was rich in the grace of God. God had purchased her and made her His own. Although she owned no possessions, Mrs. Carson said Cheryl herself was a treasured possession of God. Cheryl thought about that for a while. Soon she began to receive comfort from knowing that, at least in God's eyes, she was rich. Not only that, she was God's prized possession. That made her feel better. It also enabled Cheryl to live with hope.

A PEOPLE BELONGING TO GOD

To call believers "God's people" is a fairly common biblical way to speak of those who live through faith in Christ as God's possessions. The imagery, of course, is closely related to the *ransom* and *redemption* metaphors. While *ransom* focuses on the *price* paid and *redemption* focuses on the *act* of paying, this last commercial metaphor emphasizes the result of the transaction: We are owned by God; we are His possessions, His property.[1]

In 1 Peter 2:9, Peter affirms: "But you are a chosen people, a royal priesthood, a holy nation, a people belonging to God,

PROPERTY

that you may declare the praises of Him who called you out of
darkness into His wonderful light." This passage is a primary
source for the doctrine of the "priesthood of all believers." We
are set apart, as were Israel's ancient priests, to offer spiritual
sacrifices to God in Christ. We are also "a people belonging to
God."[2] St. Peter announces to his hearers that they are God's
possession. Elsewhere in the same letter, Peter explains the
price Christ paid to make us God's own: "not with perishable
things such as silver or gold ... but with the precious blood of
Christ, a lamb without blemish of defect" (1 Peter 1:18–19).
Paul makes a similar point when he charges the elders in Ephe-
sus: "Be shepherds of the church of God, which He bought
with His own blood" (Acts 20:28).

> "They will be Mine," says the Lord Almighty, "in the day
> when I make up My treasured possession. I will spare them,
> just as in compassion a man spares his son who serves him."
> (Malachi 3:17)

Many of the Bible passages containing the *property* metaphor also emphasize the idea of wealth or riches. In Exodus
19:5–6, God tells Moses to say to the Israelites: "If you obey Me
fully and keep My covenant, then out of all nations you will
be My treasured possession. Although the whole earth is Mine,
you will be for Me a kingdom of priests and a holy nation."
Later, God tells the Israelites: "For you are a people holy to
the Lord your God. The Lord your God has chosen you out of
all the peoples on the face of the earth to be His people, His
treasured possession" (Deuteronomy 7:6). Note the connection
between being God's possession and being treasured by God.
We receive our value from the one who owns us. Because we
are owned by God, we have infinite value.

Poor

If the Gospel is that we are purchased and owned by God
and, therefore, a treasured possession, then the Law is that we
are disowned and valueless. That's a common feeling in our

world! Many people are "down and out" financially. Bankruptcy is on the rise. People are borrowing at unprecedented rates. They're in debt. Lack of money and possessions can cause people to question their self-worth, their self-value. It doesn't matter whether their predicament is caused by their own wrong choices, by an inability to exercise self-discipline in spending, or by forces beyond their control. The end result is that people are flat broke, which usually causes emotional and psychological bankruptcy as well.

Of course, there are other ways to be broke that are even more widespread and more damaging than the lack of capital. Moral bankruptcy is everywhere as people increasingly put off the mores of the past, which contributed to a way of living that was rich with love and a sense of community. Today many people lead empty existences, valueless lifestyles, that are depleted of goodness and overdrawn on selfishness and greed.

No matter the form bankruptcy takes, it is symptomatic of a spiritual bankruptcy before God. Our lives are empty when compared to the fullness and richness of the one who created us. Our lives are valueless when seen in the light of the supreme value of the one from whom all things come.

But it is even worse than that. We are not only bankrupt, we are arrogant in our emptiness. We think we can amass enough treasures, store up enough good works, so God will favor us with His grace. We self-righteously collect our good works as if they were great treasures, imagining that we could earn God's favor. But when we look in the bank, we see that our account is empty. All our efforts have added up to zero. They merit nothing.

We become rich only as we live through faith in the one who is eternally rich. That's what Cheryl came to understand. She realized that her poverty was not a sign of evil before God. It was a symptom of a much deeper poverty, a spiritual poverty, which she and all people had before God. When she saw that, Cheryl glimpsed the great value she had as one redeemed by Christ the crucified.

Rich

What indescribably good news! Although poor materially, Cheryl was infinitely rich in God's grace. What joy and hope this gives to God's people. In Christ, through faith in Him, all of us have great value. We are God's prized possessions, His special treasure (Deuteronomy 7:6), His precious jewels (Zechariah 9:16).

Our treasury is filled to overflowing not with our good works, but with the good works of Christ, who on the cross performed the greatest, the most precious, and the most meritorious good work of all. He bought us back from our bankruptcy. He purchased us from our valueless existence. He saved us from being required to earn our redemption. He gave our redemption to us as an infinitely valuable gift.

> We wait for the blessed hope—the glorious appearing of our great God and Savior, Jesus Christ, who gave Himself for us to redeem us from all wickedness and to purify for Himself a people that are His very own, eager to do what is good. (Titus 2:13–14)

Christ did this through a great exchange: "For you know the grace of our Lord Jesus Christ, that though He was rich, yet for your sakes He became poor, so that you through His poverty might become rich" (2 Corinthians 8:9). He became poor. He entered into our poverty—not only our physical poverty, but our spiritual poverty as well. On the cross Christ took our place as poor, valueless, bankrupt individuals. He became poor so we might be rich. God has "chosen those who are poor in the eyes of the world to be rich in faith and to inherit the kingdom" (James 2:5).

God has not promised to free us from material poverty. Of course, Christians who enjoy a goodly measure of God's providential gifts always will give Him the glory. When a believer is able, by hard work, to raise herself out of material poverty, she will give the credit to God as the giver of all good things. Nevertheless, God has not promised to make each of us financially rich. That's a hard pill to swallow for those who live below the poverty line. Christians always will be moved by love to help their disadvantaged brothers and sisters. But this much is absolutely certain: Christ has made rich all those who by faith live in Him. They are His priceless treasures, the jewels in His crown, His prized possessions.

ENDNOTES

1. The Greek word translated as "possession" is *peripoiesis*.
2. The same Greek word translated as "possession" (*peripoiesis*) is translated here as "belonging."

11

Forgiveness/Remission

Forgive us our debts, as we also have forgiven our debtors. (Matthew 6:12)

UP TO OUR EYEBALLS IN DEBT

"How could this happen?" Victor yelled at Carmen. "How could *you* let this happen?"

He was taking his frustrations out on his wife, but Victor knew he was equally to blame for their troubles. They were living beyond their means, and all those credit cards didn't help. It was too easy to buy stuff. But now the bills had come, and Victor knew they were in trouble. There was no way they could repay that debt. In fact, their liabilities added up to more than half their annual income. They were up to their eyeballs in debt.

Victor and Carmen decided to get financial advice. And while they undertook an overhaul in their financial life, they determined to overhaul life in general. In addition to taking control of their finances through careful spending, they also decided it was time to go back to church. After all, the kids hadn't been in Sunday school for more than a year, and they hadn't attended church as a family for who knows how long.

As Victor, Carmen, and the kids said the Lord's Prayer that next Sunday, the familiar words "Forgive us our trespasses, as we forgive those who trespass against us" struck Victor like a slap in the face. He recalled the Spanish phrase he had memorized as a child: *"Perdona nuestras deudas, así como nosotros perdonamos a nuestros deudores."* He whispered the translation to himself as the service continued, "Forgive us our *debts,* as we forgive our *debtors."*

Victor couldn't seem to get his debts off his mind. *Wouldn't it be great if God really would cancel my debt?* Victor thought. Then he thought about what the pastor had said during the sermon: "Your debts have all been canceled, and in a manner far greater than merely paying off your bills. Your debt of sin has been canceled through the death of Jesus Christ on the cross." *What wonderful news,* Victor thought. *I am forgiven.*

Unless You Forgive Your Brother

Because it is considered a dead metaphor, the Gospel metaphor of *forgiveness* has suffered from misuse and lack of use.[1] It is understood as such a general, theological term that few people realize it is a vivid metaphor of great power. In fact, the *forgiveness* metaphor operates within two primary metaphorical worlds. First, it is a personal metaphor that denotes the rectification of a relationship gone bad.[2] Occasionally, however, this word is used in Scripture to denote the forgiveness of a debt. When used in this way, *forgiveness* becomes a commercial metaphor.

In His parable of the unmerciful servant (Matthew 18:21–35), Jesus uses *forgiveness* in its meaning of "the remission of a debt" as a primary metaphor for His work. Jesus' parable comes in answer to a question from Peter: "Lord, how many times shall I forgive my brother when he sins against me? Up to seven times?" (Matthew 18:21). Peter undoubtedly thought he was being more than generous in using seven, the number of completion. However, Jesus says, "I tell you, not seven times, but seventy-seven times" (Matthew 18:22).[3] In this way, Jesus tells Peter that true forgiveness is limitless.

Jesus then describes how a king forgives the debt of a servant who owed him what would be millions of dollars in today's currency. After being forgiven by the king, however, this servant refuses to forgive a fellow servant who owes him only a few dollars. When the king hears about it, he calls the first servant back and orders him to be jailed until he can repay his debt.

Jesus' point about forgiveness is this: "This is how My heavenly Father will treat each of you unless you forgive your brother from your heart" (Matthew 18:35). In other words, we are to forgive others as we ourselves have been forgiven. Jesus draws on vivid language in His parable. He uses a metaphor from commerce.

To enter into the kingdom of heaven, that is to enter into a living faith relationship with God, one first must have his or her debts paid. Like the first servant, we are so deeply in debt because of our sins that we could never pay God off on our own. Our only hope is that God, out of His gracious favor, will cancel our debt. And He has. The price was paid as the Son of God poured out His blood on the cross in payment to satisfy our debt.

> "Therefore, the kingdom of heaven is like a king who wanted to settle accounts with his servants. As he began the settlement, a man who owed him ten thousand talents was brought to him. Since he was not able to pay, the master ordered that he and his wife and his children and all that he had be sold to repay the debt. The servant fell on his knees before him. 'Be patient with me,' he begged, 'and I will pay back everything.' The servant's master took pity on him, canceled the debt and let him go." (Matthew 18:23–27)

Debtors

One way to look at our condition before God apart from Christ is that we are debtors. Many people understand the concept of being in debt. They know what it's like to have creditors calling at all hours of the day. They understand having things repossessed. They know the shame of filing for bankruptcy. In the past, we put debtors in the poor house or debtors' prison. Now we haul them into court and garnish their wages. The number of people who directly experience indebtedness is, unfortunately, on the rise.

Although not everyone is a debtor in this full sense, we all understand the idea of being in debt. We all know the burden of financial commitments: house payments, car payments, credit card bills. We all seem to be up to our eyeballs in debt.

But what we may not know is that these encumbrances are a dim reflection of a much greater indebtedness that we all have. We are in debt to God. We are "in hock" to God. We "owe Him big." We have sinned and grieved Him. He demands payment, but the cost is too high. We can't repay our debt. There isn't enough money in the world, even if it were proper to pay God off with money. The cost of our debt is death. We will die paupers, in debtors' prison, without hope of release.

CANCELED

Wonderfully, our debt has been canceled. That's what Victor saw. Although he and Carmen were in financial debt, their debt of sin already had been canceled through the blood of Jesus Christ. The payment was not "silver or gold," but the "precious blood of Christ, a lamb without blemish or defect" (1 Peter 1:18–19). This was a price more valuable than all the money in the world, one that fully satisfied God. Our almighty God accepted the blood of the Lamb as payment in full for the sins of the entire world. What good news! And what an interesting way to say it: Our debt to God has been canceled; we are forgiven.

God does not promise to pay off all our financial debts. Those who claim that God promises property and a debt-free life are chasing a dream. Like Victor and Carmen, we exercise discipline in our financial stewardship because it is not easy to put our financial lives back together. But the hardest part already has been done as a free gift. Before God, we are debt-free. Knowing this gives us strength and courage to face the future in the sure hope that because of the blood of the Lamb, we are forgiven.

ENDNOTES

1. The Greek word translated as "forgiveness" is *aphesis*.
2. See "Part 5: Christ the Reconciler: Personal Metaphors."
3. The NIV footnote correctly provides an alternate rendering as "*seventy times seven.*"

PART 4

CHRIST THE JUDGE: LEGAL METAPHORS

12

Justification

Therefore, since we have been justified through faith, we have peace with God through our Lord Jesus Christ, through whom we have gained access by faith into this grace in which we now stand. And we rejoice in the hope of the glory of God. (Romans 5:1–2)

FEELING GUILTY

Christian was worried about his friend. Jim was always so hard on himself. He blamed himself for everything, even things that obviously were not his fault. Jim once told Christian that he felt guilty for not caring for his family as well as he should have, guilty for not spending as much time with his children as he should have, guilty for not being as successful at work as he should have. Jim seemed always to carry a load of guilt, which affected his sense of well-being as well as his personal relationships.

Christian didn't know how to help his friend. Jim was a nice guy who had never done anything really wrong. It wasn't right that he should feel so guilty all the time.

One day while reading his Bible, Christian came across Romans 5:9, which read: "Since we have now been justified by His blood, how much more shall we be saved from God's wrath through Him!" Christian read the study note at the bottom of the page, which said that *justified* is a courtroom term. St. Paul was writing that no charge can be brought against God's people because God already has pronounced the verdict: *not guilty.*

Immediately, Christian thought of Jim. He couldn't wait to tell his friend that in God's eyes he was not guilty. Jesus had taken Jim's guilt—and the guilt of the entire world—to Himself when He died on the cross. Through faith in Christ, we are no longer guilty; God declares us *not guilty.* No one can bring a charge against us.

THE RIGHTEOUSNESS OF GOD THROUGH FAITH

It is difficult to overstate the importance of the legal metaphors for the full proclamation of the Gospel. During the time of the Reformation, Martin Luther and the other reformers called the church of the 16th-century back to its biblical and evangelical roots primarily on the basis of the restoration of the legal metaphors and the language of justification. This articulation of the Gospel became central to the entire Reformation and even lent its name to the article of faith that gave rise to the necessary reform: the doctrine of justification by faith. On purely historical grounds, therefore, one could hardly overemphasize this way of saying the Gospel.

Apart from these historical considerations, the legal metaphors are vital to the Gospel because they add an element that cannot be clearly gained from any other metaphor. The legal metaphors, particularly *justification,*[1] bring an objectivity that is absolutely essential to a full understanding of the Gospel.[2] In short, the legal metaphors make it clear that the first and most important aspect of Christ's work for us is that He *set things right* with God. Thus, the first and primary work that happens occurs outside of us and in God.

Although *justification* is found in many New Testament writings, the word is unquestionably a favorite of St. Paul. In fact, nearly all of the language of justification comes from his writings. Jesus used the word only a handful of times. (See Matthew 5:6; 6:33.) It has powerful testimony in the Old Testament too. Many messianic prophecies speak of a "righteous judge" who will come and exercise justice. (See Isaiah 46:13; 53:11; Jeremiah 23:5–6.)

Although *justification* is a dominant metaphor in Paul's writings, it is the central argument of the Epistle to the Romans. The foundational text for this metaphor is Romans 3:21–28. Paul uses several Gospel metaphors in this passage, but the legal one dominates:

> But now a righteousness [or *justification*] of God, apart from Law, has been made known.... This righteousness of God comes through faith in Jesus Christ to all who believe. There is no difference, for all have sinned and fall short of the glory of God, and are justified freely by His grace. (Romans 3:21–24)

Paul says that a person is declared righteous or just by God in the legal sense (that is, not guilty of crimes) on the basis of God's grace, on account of Jesus Christ, apart from works of the Law. Although the Law was given by God as a good and gracious gift (Romans 3:1–2), the doing of the Law cannot accomplish anything in God's eyes because "all have sinned and fall short of the glory of God" (Romans 3:23). No one can fulfill the Law perfectly as God requires. Thus, everyone is guilty before God. In fact, apart from faith, the Law only increases a sinner's consciousness of sin (Romans 3:19).

Standing against all human accomplishment or claim on God is the righteousness of God that comes through faith. This is a justice, first of all, which is God's very own. What Paul describes is not merely the righteousness that God requires of His sinful creatures. More important, it is a righteousness that God Himself gives to those who believe in His only Son, Jesus Christ. The righteousness that justifies is precisely God's very own justice. He gives it to us by declaring us, as a Judge would, "Not guilty."

Faith stands over and against all human righteousness and good works. Faith is purely passive and receptive. Faith is not another good work we do that causes God to declare us just.[3] Rather, faith is more of a receptive instrument through which God bestows His righteousness on us. In other words, faith is an "instrumental means" through which we come into possession of God's righteousness. Furthermore, faith is more properly defined according to its object than its subject. This means that the quality of faith is defined not by the one doing the believing, but by the one who is believed. Faith saves because of its object!

Paul follows his extended discussion of the "justification of God" in Romans 3 by setting forth an historical precedent. In Romans 4, Paul discusses the primary Old Testament example of justification by faith. Quoting Genesis 15:6, Paul affirms: "Abraham believed God, and it was credited to him as righteousness." Against all hope (Abraham was about 100 years old), contrary to all the evidence (Sarah's womb was "also dead"), Abraham believed the promise that he would become the father of many nations (Romans 4:18–21).

> The words "it was credited to him" were written not for him alone, but also for us, to whom God will credit righteousness—for us who believe in Him who raised Jesus our Lord from the dead. He was delivered over to death for our sins and was raised to life for our justification. (Romans 4:23–25)

Abraham trusted in God's promise—he was forced to because there was certainly no basis for hoping in himself—and God regarded him as righteous. God *credited* trust to Abraham as righteousness. The word *credited*[4] has the force of being understood as "reckoning, crediting, or regarding." Paul draws attention to the one doing the reckoning, not to the one being reckoned. It is forensic, legal language in the sense that Abraham's righteousness was really God's righteousness. The reality of Abraham's righteousness is in the one who does the reckoning, not in the one reckoned. This is powerfully objective. The burden of our justification rests—all of it—on God.

Thus, the reality of justification is not in the one justified, but in the one who justifies; not in the recipient, but in the Giver; not in being made just, but in declaring just.

One unfortunate result of the centrality to the Reformation of the legal metaphors is that the language became highly charged theologically and took on technical meaning. This, of course, was unavoidable and even necessary. However, it has caused people to forget that this is metaphorical language. It is language borrowed from the courtroom. It evokes an entire realm of thought and ideas. It brings to mind legal codes, crimes, courts of law, lawyers, judges, pleas, convictions, defenses, verdicts, and a host of other associations with which people can readily identify. The language is richly textured and vivid. At times it triggers strong associations. It is imperative that we hear this Gospel language in its relation to its legal roots.

THE WAGES OF SIN

In light of a Gospel metaphor that sees sinners as declared not guilty by a righteous judge, how does one experience the Law? The primary experience, of course, is guilt. Nearly everyone can relate to this, even if we never have been in court— even traffic court. Television is filled with images of the law: lawyers, judges, juries, opening statements, evidence, and verdicts. Shows such as *Perry Mason, L.A. Law, People's Court, Law and Order,* and *The Practice* are just a few of the popular dramas that have brought the courtroom into our homes. We know the vocabulary: defendant, witness, "your honor." Nearly everyone in the western world can relate to the notions of guilt and innocence that come out of the courtroom.

For some, of course, the experience of the Law comes in the form of a real "brush with the law." People are guilty of, or are charged with, some actual legal infraction. They know firsthand what it is to be dragged into a courtroom and charged with a crime. They know how it is to be treated as a criminal, to face a judge, to be confused and scared in the face of a mystifying legal system, to make a plea, to be convicted of a crime, to receive a sentence, to be punished. They know the "long arm of the law."

For others, the experience is not so direct or dramatic, but it is equally troubling. They experience guilt in a vague, general manner. Like Jim, they have an undefined sense of being "guilty" that lacks focus. Jim couldn't identify the cause—he had not actually murdered someone or stolen someone's property. Instead, he had a vague sense of guilt that he couldn't attach to some firm action or inaction on his part.

Other people feel no sense of guilt. They feel no responsibility for situations they did not directly cause. They understand the law in a purely formal sense—they are guilty only if they commit an actual infraction. Others "justify" their behavior because "everyone does it."

But everyone needs to understand—those who are actually guilty of breaking the law, those who merely feel guilty, and those who do not feel guilty—that their guilt is *theological*. Infractions of the laws of the state are merely a window into the more serious infraction of God's Law. The feelings of guilt are symptomatic of the much more profound transgression of the laws of God. Those who do not feel guilty and have no sense of their guilt are deluding themselves. Everyone is guilty. As Paul says, "There is no one righteous, not even one" (Romans 3:10). This is more than a feeling. It is actual guilt before the righteous Judge of all.

There is, however, a danger implicit in understanding our "problem" as an infraction of God's Law. We believe our problem is that we have violated some impersonal code of laws or ethics. This is not the case. When we transgress God's commands, we transgress God Himself. What is wrong with going against God's Law is that the Law reflects God Himself. To violate the command is to violate God. It is an affront not merely to the code, but to the person of God. He is the one who enacts the laws, the one who enforces them, the one who tries lawbreakers, and the one who judges them.

God plays all the parts in this courtroom drama except one: the accused. *You* are on trial. All the evidence is brought against you. You don't have a legal leg to stand on. God has you "dead to rights." He will "throw the book at you." The case against you is so serious, so conclusive, that you have no defense. In fact, you are guilty not of breaking a few of God's laws, but of breaking *all* of His laws. James 2:10 reads: "Whoever keeps the whole Law and yet stumbles at just one point is guilty of breaking all of it." You have no recourse but to throw yourself on the mercy of the court. Your guilt is apparent to all. Your conviction is certain. Your punishment will be severe: "The wages of sin is death" (Romans 6:23).

NOT GUILTY!

As people guilty before the righteous Judge, the verdict of *not guilty* can be heard only as the greatest good news. How wonderful! Although all your thoughts, words, and deeds make you "guilty as sin" before God, on account of Christ you are acquitted. God declares you to be not guilty of any crimes of which you had been charged. The case is closed. Court is adjourned. You are free to go. This is not because God ignored the crimes. It is because He exacted the punishment against His own innocent Son. Christ suffered the wages of sin in our place.

Paul says it this way in Romans 8:1–2: "Therefore, there is now no condemnation for those who are in Christ Jesus, because through Christ Jesus the law of the Spirit of life set me free from the law of sin and death." A sentence different from the one we deserved has been handed down. We deserved condemnation and death. Instead, on account of Christ and because He perfectly fulfilled the Law in every respect, we have been sentenced to life and freedom. Our innocence is not really ours, but Christ's. It has been imputed, that is, it has been credited or reckoned to us by God through faith. Christ's obedience to the Law is now ours. Thus, our righteousness is both perfect and full, just like Christ's. Paul says that our righteousness is God's very own because our sin is exchanged for the perfect righteousness of Christ (2 Corinthians 5:21). What indescribable good news! We are declared—and, therefore, we are—not guilty.

> "We who are Jews by birth and not 'Gentile sinners' know that a man is not justified by observing the Law, but by faith in Jesus Christ. So we, too, have put our faith in Christ Jesus that we may be justified by faith in Christ and not by observing the Law, because by observing the Law no one will be justified." (Galatians 2:15–16)

The Bible speaks of God's judgment both as a past and a future event. The day of judgment is in the past. It is the day when God declared His Son's obedience to the Law sufficient for the justification of the world. At the same time, Paul writes, "Now there is in store for me the crown of righteousness, which the Lord, the righteous Judge, will award to me on that day" (2 Timothy 4:8). Which is it? Past or future? It's both. In the past, God declared Himself satisfied with the obedience of Christ. His saving work is sufficient for the guilt of the entire world. However, we receive God's righteousness now by faith. One day, our full justification will be revealed for the entire world to see and we will live in "righteousness and innocence and blessedness" with our Lord for all eternity. On Judgment Day, our Lord will announce publicly the judgment He made in the past at the cross and the judgment He makes in the present each time that He, by His Word, declares the sinner just through faith in Jesus Christ.

ENDNOTES

1. The Greek word for "justify" and "justification" is *dikaioo*.
2. In English, we have two translations of *dikaiosune*: *justification* and *righteousness*. Although they may have slightly different connotations in English, both words come from the same Greek word and should be given the same meaning. It is

unclear why translators choose one or the other word to translate the same root. The only difference between them is that they have come to English via different routes. *Righteousness* comes from the German *Rechtfertigung*, and *justification* comes from the Latin *iustitia*.

3. In a certain sense, faith is the primary and first of all good works, as Martin Luther often said. However, it must be kept clear that the power of faith, as well as its goodness, lies not in the one doing the believing, but in the one who is believed, that is, in faith's object.

4. The Greek word translated as "credited" is *logesthai*.

13

Intercession

Who will bring any charge against those whom God has chosen? It is God who justifies. Who is he that condemns? Christ Jesus, who died—more than that, who was raised to life—is at the right hand of God and is also interceding for us. (Romans 8:33–34)

DEFENSELESS

Jane felt alone in the world. Her marriage had ended in divorce. Now she had two young children to care for, which meant a struggle to make ends meet. What bothered her most, however, was feeling as though she had no one to speak for her, no one to take her side. The loneliness didn't bother her. She was content with herself, and she loved her children. But this business of facing the world alone, of having no one to speak for her, no one to act as her advocate, made her uncomfortable.

At church the next Sunday, Jane's pastor read from Romans 8. From her own recent experience with charges and countercharges, Jane understood the apostle Paul's imagery. But the last part of the text captured her heart: "Christ is interceding for us" (Romans 8:34). That was exactly what she had needed—someone to stand beside her, like a defense lawyer, and plead her case! Jesus was that someone who stood by her, mediated for her, comforted her with His wise counsel. Jane had never thought of it like that before.

INTERCEDING FOR US

The idea that Christ is our intercessor or mediator is closely related to justification. The metaphor still "swims within the pool" of the courtroom and law. The difference is that our intercessor, Christ, takes the role of our defense lawyer, while in the *justification* metaphor, God had been primarily in the role of judge. Although the two metaphors share a similar context, they deserve to be treated separately. However, much of what was said in the previous section about the objectivity and the forensic character of the legal metaphors also applies here.

Intercession is an interesting metaphor because it rounds out the picture of the courtroom and adds a necessary dimension to the legal metaphors. We have seen that God is the accuser, the judge, and the executioner. The sinner stands defenseless against overwhelming and damning evidence. Now, however, we see that we are not defenseless as we stand before the bar of justice. Christ is our defense.

Several different words used to describe Jesus' role in this regard are found in Scripture. At times, Christ is spoken of as the one who intercedes (Romans 8:34; Hebrews 7:25). Sometimes He is the one who takes up our cause and pleads our case before a judge. At other times, Jesus serves as the mediator between two disputing parties or litigants (1 Timothy 2:5; Galatians 3:19–20). Still other times, Jesus is spoken of as a "counselor for the defense" who provides comfort and advice for the accused (1 John 2:1). This, too, is rich and varied language that provides us with profound insight into the role our Lord played to bring us to acquittal for our transgressions.

> The LORD looked and was displeased that there was no justice. He saw that there was no one, He was appalled that there was no one to intervene; so His own arm worked salvation

for him, and His own righteousness sustained him. (Isaiah
5:15b–16)

WITHOUT ONE PLEA

The malady behind *intercession* is a bit different than that
behind *justification*. In the *justification* metaphor, we stood
guilty before a holy Law and a righteous Judge, but God justified us. Another look at this courtroom picture shows that we
also are defenseless. As defendants we are guilty as we stand
before the Judge. He has us "dead to rights." As the accused,
we have no one to plead our case. We don't even know how to
plead because we aren't fully aware of our guilt or the charges.
The complicated, mysterious legal system and its intimidating
legal code and lawyers compound the guilt the accused feel
with a sense of fear.

Many people can relate to this metaphor, even if they
never have had a negative experience with the legal system.
Most people feel that they have no one to come to their aid, no
one to be their advocate and speak for them, no one to provide
wise counsel. Such feelings may have no specific connection
with the legal system, but they are related to a widespread
sense of lack of direction. People feel that they face a cruel,
accusing world all alone without anyone to defend them, just
as Jane felt. She needed someone to stand with her. She needed
a defender.

What Jane didn't know, however, was just how serious
her problem was. She was not just without counsel against the
world, her real problem was her defenselessness before God.
She and all people apart from faith in Christ are "hauled into
court" to face a righteous Judge—God. He is angry because of
our infraction of His Law and our offense to Him. Our feelings
of being without an advocate are merely a symbol of our much
greater defenselessness before our God.

Counselor for the Defense

Because of her feelings of defenselessness, Jane was intrigued when she heard Jesus referred to as her "intercessor." She heard this as the answer to her need. For people who feel as though no one will come to their defense, there is good news! Christ is with us. He stands beside us before the judge. He pleads our case. A wise counselor, Jesus knows just what to say. He has our defense strategy planned. He has written a brief. He has prepared opening and closing statements. He will defend us to the fullest extent of the law.

> My dear children, I write this to you so that you will not sin. But if anybody does sin, we have one who speaks to the Father in our defense—Jesus Christ, the Righteous One. (1 John 2:1–2)

Jesus' defense is this: He stands in our place. He is convicted for our crimes, punished for our offenses. He takes the death penalty on the cross so we might receive a pardon, a stay of execution, for our crimes. He is, incredibly, much more than our legal counsel. He actually takes our place, fully identifying with our plight. He is in the fullest sense our *paraclete,* standing with us before the Judge to receive in our place the verdict we deserve. Jesus places Himself between us and our accuser, between us and certain death. Punishment is averted, a death sentence commuted. What wonderful news! We do not face the world—cold and accusing—alone. Standing beside us is Jesus—our advocate, intercessor, counselor, comforter, defender, and mediator.

Even now, Jesus continues to be our intercessor. Because He wants to bring to completion the justification He earned for us, He continues to intercede for us in heaven before the Father (Hebrews 7:25). And He has given us "another Counselor" (John 14:16), who, while Jesus pleads our case in heaven, continues His comforting presence with us, reminding us of everything Jesus has said (John 14:26). Jesus has poured out on us His Holy Spirit, who now through the Word serves as

Christ's presence among us and provides us with the effective counsel we need. In this way, Jesus continues to stand beside us as we face the trials of life. We are not alone. Christ, our counselor, is with us.

14

Adoption

Praise be to the God and Father of our Lord Jesus Christ, who has blessed us in the heavenly realms with every spiritual blessing in Christ. For He chose us in Him before the creation of the world to be holy and blameless in His sight. In love He predestined us to be adopted as His sons through Jesus Christ, in accordance with His pleasure and will—to the praise of His glorious grace, which He has freely given us in the One He loves. (Ephesians 1:3–6)

WHO AM I?

Throughout his 20 years of life, Mark had been bothered by the question of his own identity. He really didn't know who he was. He had known from the beginning that he was adopted; he was Asian while his parents were white. He was happy with his adopted family because he knew he was loved. And he certainly had been cared for more than adequately.

But Mark felt like he didn't really know who he was because he didn't know who his biological parents were. All Mark knew was that he had been given up for adoption at an early age and that he had an older brother. His mother, the agency reported, had been unable to care for the boys. Mark could remember nothing from his life before his adoption. He drew his entire sense of identity from his adoptive parents and their other children. But the question of who he was seemed to require an answer. He wanted to find a way to reconnect with his biological family.

During the weekly Bible study he attended at the university chapel, Mark heard something strange. The leader was reading from Ephesians: "In love He predestined us to be adopted as His sons through Jesus Christ, in accordance with His pleasure and will" (Ephesians 1:4–5). It was the reference to adoption that caught Mark's attention. *I've been adopted by my parents and given a new family. Is that what has happened because of my faith in Christ?* Mark asked himself. *Have I become a member of God's family and been given a new identity, God's identity?* Mark had never thought of his faith in that way before.

THE SPIRIT OF SONSHIP

Adoption is an interesting metaphor because it evokes a more personal touch in addition to its strong legal connotations.[1] It is, first of all, a legal metaphor, both in the biblical world and in our modern world. Adoption was, and still is, something that takes place in a courtroom and is formalized by a judge. One is legally declared to be another's child in a court of law. The *adoption* metaphor, then, has all the objective implications of the other legal metaphors. However, adoption is personal because a new relationship is formed in which one is given a legal family where there was not one before. *Adoption* is a bridge between the legal and the personal metaphors. It emphasizes the process through which we become children of God (a legal process), but it also reveals the new relationship between parents and children.

In several significant passages (Romans 8:15–23; Galatians 3:26–4:7), Paul explores this way of speaking the Gospel. The Galatians passage is particularly instructive. Paul asserts that those who have been baptized into Christ are "sons of God."

We stand in a loving and favorable relationship with the Father. The process of adoption brought about this "sonship." By nature, we were slaves, that is, not God's children. We were the children of the "basic principles of the world" (Ephesians 4:3), evil forces that enslaved and oppressed us. But when the time had fully come, God "sent His son, born of a woman, born under Law, to redeem those under Law, that we might receive the full rights of sons" (Ephesians 4:4–5).[2]

> For you did not receive a spirit that makes you a slave again to fear, but you received the Spirit of sonship. And by Him we cry, "Abba, Father." The Spirit Himself testifies with our spirit that we are God's children. Now if we are children, then we are heirs—heirs of God and co-heirs with Christ, if indeed we share in His sufferings in order that we may also share in His glory. (Romans 8:15–17)

We are, as it were, taken away from our evil "biological parents" and given by adoption to be the children of God. This happened as the true Son of God (Son not by adoption, but because He is "the only-begotten Son," "begotten of His Father before all worlds;" *Nicene Creed*) took our place "under Law," that is, under the "basic principles of the world." As a result, God has given the "Spirit of His Son" into our hearts, enabling us to call God *Abba*, that is, *Father*. We are now God's children by adoption, loved and protected by our Father. As Paul says, we are no longer slaves but beloved sons and daughters in God's family.

ORPHANS

In light of this Gospel metaphor, how does one experience the Law? We are orphans, cut off from our rightful, "biological" Father. Many people can relate to being orphans—parentless, abandoned, separated from the love and nurture a parent gives to a child. Those who have been adopted know something of the uncertainty or incompleteness that comes from being separated from one's natural parents. Although adoption was the right thing to do and has been a blessing, people like Mark still suffer because they don't know the whole story of who they are. Even those who are not physically separated from parents can suffer emotional and physical abuse or abandonment, which can be more painful than being an orphan. All of these people experience directly what it is like to be cut off from one's parents.

Others feel "orphaned" in another sense. They feel a sense of incompleteness, of not being fully who they are. They ask "Who am I?" "Where do I belong?" "What is my purpose in life?" These questions point to a relationship far more basic and important than an earthly relationship. They point to our relationship to God. They point to the fact that something is not right between God and us. Our feelings of being cut off point to the fact that we are cut off from God. We don't know who we are and we never will know our identity because in our sinful waywardness we have separated ourselves from the only one we could call Father. We are the abused children of an evil and unworthy parent; we are "objects of wrath" (Ephesians 2:3).

ADOPTED CHILDREN

This reality is behind Mark's search for himself, though he was unaware of it. His search ended, however, when he discovered that, through faith in Christ, he had been adopted by his loving heavenly Father. Through Baptism, God has gathered His disparate creatures and brought them into His household. He has adopted us, declared us to be His children. Now we know who we are because we know whose we are. Now we are cherished, wanted, desired, acknowledged by our Father. Now we have the full rights of children. No longer are we slaves of an evil taskmaster, objects of wrath. Now we know that God loves us. Because we know this, we may now live as children of God, as those born of God.

> So also, when we were children, we were in slavery under the basic principles of the world. But when the time had fully come, God sent His Son, born of a woman, born under Law, to redeem those under Law, that we might receive the full

rights of sons. Because you are sons, God sent the Spirit of His Son into our hearts, the Spirit who calls out, *"Abba,* Father." So you are no longer a slave, but a son; and since you are a son, God has made you also an heir. (Galatians 4:3–7)

ENDNOTES

1. The Greek word translated as "adoption" is *huiothesia.*
2. The NIV translation "full rights of sons" also may be translated as "adoption as sons."

15

Inheritance

And we pray this in order that you may live a life worthy of the Lord and may please Him in every way: bearing fruit in every good work, growing in the knowledge of God, being strengthened with all power according to His glorious might so that you may have great endurance and patience, and joyfully giving thanks to the Father, who has qualified you to share in the inheritance of the saints in the kingdom of light. For He has rescued us from the dominion of darkness and brought us into the kingdom of the Son He loves. (Colossians 1:10–13)

LAST WILL AND TESTAMENT

Candy was stunned. She couldn't believe her father had done this. He always had been a difficult person, but this time he had gone too far. He had cut her out of his will. Although he had threatened to do this many times before, she never thought he would go through with it.

Candy knew she could have done more to smooth things over with her father. She knew she had done many things to upset him. Her lifestyle was, perhaps, a little on the "loose" side. But it was her life to live. Her father didn't own her. Still,

Candy had come to depend too much on her parents' generosity. What would she do now?

When Candy told her friend Jan about everything, Jan said something interesting. Jan had been attending a singles' Bible study at her church and had been struck by the passage: "Now if we are children, then we are heirs—heirs of God and co-heirs with Christ, if indeed we share in His sufferings in order that we may also share in His glory" (Romans 8:17). That sounded strange to Candy. Was it possible that she could be an heir of God, even though her parents had disinherited her? Could she be disowned by her father and owned by God? She decided to look into this business about Jesus again.

An Imperishable Inheritance

An important aspect of the legal metaphors for the Gospel is the cluster of ideas surrounding *inheritance*.[1] This is a significant category in Scripture, both quantitatively and qualitatively. Because inheritance has to do with wills and testaments, we see the clear connection to legal language. Like *adoption,* however, *inheritance* also serves as a bridge to the personal metaphors because it also has a great deal to do with relationships.

Inheritance is closely linked in Scripture with adoption. In Galatians 3:26–4:7, Paul outlines our hope in Christ as children of God. Our release from slavery "under the basic principles of the world" and our adoption as sons lead immediately to the conclusion, "So you are no longer a slave, but a son; and since you are a son, God has made you also an heir" (Galatians 4:7). Having been made legally God's children through adoption, we now come into possession of His entire "estate" by receiving an inheritance.

In 1 Peter 1:3–5, the apostle writes:

In His great mercy He has given us new birth into a living hope through the resurrection of Jesus Christ from the dead, and into an inheritance that can never perish, spoil or fade—kept in heaven for you, who through faith are shielded by God's power until the coming of the salvation that is ready to be revealed in the last time.

Peter does not explicitly mention adoption, but he uses the more general "new birth" to establish that those who have faith in Christ are children of God. Because they are children, they also are heirs. Peter focuses on the nature or character of our inheritance. First, it is indestructible. It can "never perish, spoil or fade" as other inheritances. Through faith in Christ, we come into an inheritance that will never pass away, never run out, never be exhausted.

As a result, this divine inheritance is "kept in heaven." There is a future, eschatological, dimension to the inheritance of the saints (Ephesians 1:14; Colossians 3:24; Romans 8:17). While it is necessary, as Paul does, to speak of our inheritance in the present tense, it also is necessary to speak of it in the future. It is ours now, but it will be, as Peter says, "revealed in the last time" (1 Peter 1:5).

DISOWNED

The malady to which the *inheritance* metaphor speaks as Gospel is common. It applies to anyone who, like Candy, has actually been disowned. In fact, many people are cut off from their families. They are disinherited. Those who have experienced this know the hurt and the pain it can cause. We tend to think of ourselves as independent, as going our own way, but attachment to family and the sense of belonging, security, and identity that family brings remains strong. Family is a powerful force, even in the lives of those who, for one reason or another, are legally cut off from parents, siblings, or children. To be "cut out of the will" is a serious and painful business.

Of course, people can be disowned in ways that are not legal, but which cause the same amount of personal suffering. A sad reality of our times is that people routinely cut themselves off from one another, "disinheriting one another."

These situations may lack the legal and financial dimension, but they produce the same results: Family members do not talk to one another and act like virtual strangers, even while living under the same roof. This, in fact, was what Candy found most troubling. Certainly she would miss the money and support and the legal protection afforded by a will. But she would miss most the contact with her father, whom she loved and whom she hoped still loved her.

All these examples are a window into a much greater disinheritance. Because of our sinfulness and waywardness, because of our "slavery" to the ways of this world, our Father in heaven disowns us. He "cuts us out of His will," unwilling even to know us. Kicked out of the house, we are left on our own to fend for ourselves and to support ourselves. We are unable to do this, of course, so we sell ourselves to the highest bidder and end up in slavery.

> This mystery is that through the Gospel the Gentiles are heirs together with Israel, members together of one body, and sharers together in the promise in Christ Jesus. (Ephesians 3:6)

HEIRS!

But through faith in Christ, we have received a different spirit—the Spirit of sonship. We are given what we don't deserve: an inheritance. We are brought into the family and made heirs. We have the full rights of family membership, including the legal right to inherit the kingdom of heaven. What an inheritance! It is imperishable. It will last forever. It will never be depleted. It will never run out or be used up. It is a heavenly "estate" made all the more secure because it is perfectly "legal."

This inheritance also is ours to use *now*. We do not have to wait until the Last Day to take advantage of our inheritance. We may draw on its benefits now. On that day when Christ returns, we will enter into the full, uninterrupted enjoyment of our heavenly riches. Until that day, however, our Lord richly and daily provides us with a foretaste of our heavenly inheritance as He provides in His Word and sacraments—all that we need to continue to be His children. What a great blessing! "An inheritance that can never perish, spoil or fade—kept in heaven for you."

ENDNOTE

1. The Greek word translated as "inheritance" is *kleronomia*.

PART 5

CHRIST THE RECONCILER: PERSONAL METAPHORS

16

Reconciliation

For He Himself is our peace, who has made the two one and has destroyed the barrier, the dividing wall of hostility, by abolishing in His flesh the Law with its commandments and regulations. His purpose to create in Himself one new man out of the two, thus making peace, and in this one body to reconcile both of them to God through the cross, by which He put to death their hostility. (Ephesians 2:14–16)

The Dividing Wall

Craig wasn't sure he could handle this. It wasn't enough that he had to work with minorities, but now an African American was his supervisor. He knew that it wasn't right to feel this way. He had been taught in Sunday school that all people were equal in God's sight and that no one person was better than another.

Based on his personal experience, Craig had no reason to think poorly of his new supervisor, but he did, and he didn't know why. It must have been his upbringing. Craig just didn't like blacks. Craig knew he needed to deal with the situation. He couldn't quit his job. He was not skilled in other fields, and he couldn't easily get another job. What could he do?

Craig's wife, Jean, suggested that he talk to their pastor, whom Craig respected. Pastor Singleton described the racial and ethnic division between Jews and Gentiles in biblical times. He then pointed out a key verse in Paul's letter to the Ephesians: "For He Himself is our peace, who has made the two one and has destroyed the barrier, the dividing wall of hostility" (2:14).

Pastor Singleton said that all who have faith in Christ are one. There is no distinction among Christians. Christ died for all and reconciled all. Craig couldn't remember ever hearing anything like that before. *If there is no difference between me and African Americans in the church, why should there be a difference at the shop?* he thought. *If race and skin color don't matter to God, they shouldn't matter to me either.*

RECONCILING THE WORLD

Another effective way to say the Gospel in Scripture is through personal metaphors. Personal metaphors borrow from the realm of relationships to say what Christ has done for us. They have to do with divisions that are healed, conflicts that are resolved, and separations that are reconciled. These metaphors emphasize forgiveness, unity, love, and relationship. For this reason, they are not only common, but they are uncommonly meaningful ways of communicating the Gospel in our day.

Everyone knows about interpersonal relationships, regardless of culture, age group, gender, or race. Personal metaphors are truly universal. Basic to this group of metaphors is the concept of reconciliation.[1] We continue to use this term in marriage relationships. When couples experience difficulties, they may separate. When they reunite, we celebrate reconciliation. The word also is used, though less often, to describe the positive outcome of a dispute between litigants or between sides in a management/labor disagreement. We say the sides are "reconciled" when they come to an agreement and the dispute ends. Reconciliation is basic to all human relationships.

Whatever causes people to take sides, whether as individuals or as groups of individuals, is overcome through reconciliation.

In the Bible, *reconciliation* is used primarily in connection with relationships between groups of peoples, that is, ethnic groups. It is a common theme in Paul's letters because a great deal of Paul's time was spent mediating disputes between people, especially between Jews and Gentiles.[2] One passage is particularly important.

> All this is from God, who reconciled us to Himself through Christ and gave us the ministry of reconciliation: that God was reconciling the world to Himself in Christ, not counting men's sins against them. And He has committed to us the message of reconciliation. (2 Corinthians 5:18–19)

Paul's primary purpose in writing these words was to support his own ministry among the Corinthians. He acknowledges that God Himself had given this ministry to Paul. In the process, however, Paul proclaims several important facts about reconciliation. First, it is God who reconciles. He "reconciled us to Himself," or as Paul says later, God "was reconciling the world to Himself." Between people, reconciliation is a two-way street. But it is not so with *God's* reconciliation of the world. God is the subject; we are always the objects. He reconciles us. We are passive. In fact, according to our natural inclinations, we are hostile and enemies of God (Romans 5:9–10). God does *all* the work of reconciling.

God performs this reconciliation through the historical work of Jesus Christ at the cross. Paul uses the past tense, "God who reconciled us to Himself through Christ." The reference is to a specific action in the past. God does not just reconcile us in general, but He reconciles us specifically because of the atonement of Christ in His active and passive obedience, that is, His fulfilling of the Law in our place and His suffering and death for our guilt. Christ's work is the cause of God's reconciliation.

The all-inclusive nature of this metaphor—its cosmic scope[3]—shines through Paul's words. More than perhaps any other Gospel metaphor, *reconciliation* reflects the universal aspect of Christ's work. It is for all, for every human being. Even those who are enemies and hostile to God have been reconciled to Him through the saving work of Christ on the cross. Of course, no one is saved apart from faith in Christ. Faith is necessary to appropriate the reconciliation of Christ. However, our faith does not make Christ's work effective. It is effective even if no one ever believes it, even if no one is saved, that is, established in heaven. Thus, though faith is necessary for salvation, the whole world already has been reconciled to God because of Christ.[4]

ALIENATION

If the Gospel is that God has reconciled us to Himself, then the Law is that we were separated—alienated—from Him. This alienation is felt everywhere by everyone. No one is exempt from alienation. Its universality grows out of the difference God has wondrously built into His creation. We are different from one another. We have different genders, races, ethnicities, ages, sizes, abilities, families, interests, occupations, and a hundred other distinctions that mark each of us as unique. However, the diversity that God created as a good, we have, through our sinfulness, turned into something that divides us. Rather than rejoicing in God's diversity, we view others who differ from us with suspicion, ignorance, and even hatred.

We have separated ourselves from one another in many ways. One truly sad reality in the history of the western world, particularly of the United States, is that race has become the focal point for hatred and fear. We have built a great wall of division between the races—a wall that has social, cultural, and economic aspects. Whatever its makeup, however, no one can ignore the impenetrable wall that has been erected between the races, particularly between blacks and whites. Craig felt it. And like so many others, he felt unable to overcome the wall between himself and his coworkers primarily because he didn't know the reasons behind its construction.

What Craig and millions of others like him do not know is that the fractures and divisions that exist between people are only a dim image of a much deeper division, a much more profound and disturbing separation, a primal alienation. Alienation exists between the Creator and His creatures. We have separated ourselves from God. We have grieved and wounded Him through our sin and our hostility toward Him.[5]

As a result of our sinful nature, we are at war with God. As His enemies, we fight against Him with all our might. We have dug a hole so deep, we have erected a wall so high, that we could never climb our way back to God. Unless there is divine intervention, we would be alienated from God forever.

At-one-ment

But God has intervened in Christ. He has reconciled us to Himself, breaking down the "dividing wall of hostility" (Ephesians 2:14). He has opened the way for rapprochement. He has taught us the proper spelling and pronunciation of that beautiful theological word *at-one-ment*. God is at one with us on account of Christ. Our alienation has been removed. We are at one with our heavenly Father, united with God. What Christ brought about through His suffering and death is unity with God. We are one with God through faith in Christ. We are no longer separated; the division has been healed. We are reconciled. Our God, Immanuel, comes to be with us, to dwell with us, to make His home with us and in us (1 Corinthians 3:16).

> For if, when we were God's enemies, we were reconciled to Him through the death of His Son, how much more, having been reconciled, shall we be saved through His life! Not only is this so, but we also rejoice in God through our Lord Jesus Christ, through whom we have now received reconciliation. (Romans 5:10–11)

Jesus brought about reconciliation by suffering separation from His Father for us. On the cross He was torn from His Father's bosom. "My God, My God! Why have You forsaken Me?" He cried from the cross. He stood in our place, across the chasm, on the other side of the wall. He endured God's hostility. He was at enmity with God. He was punished with the pains and torments of hell itself. He did this for us so we might be reconciled to the Father.

Now reconciled with God, the way has been cleared for us to be reconciled with one another. Paul makes this point in Ephesians 2:15: "His purpose was to create in Himself one new man out of the two [Jew and Gentile], thus making peace." A unity also has been brought about between people: "There is neither Jew nor Greek, slave nor free, male nor female, for you are all one in Christ Jesus" (Galatians 3:28). Through faith in Christ, we are all one. There is no distinction in God's eyes.

But what becomes of our distinctions, our differences? Are they eliminated? No. Instead of sources of division and hatred, our differences become sources of blessed diversity and joyful celebration. Because our primary alienation from God has been reconciled, we have a unity with our fellow Christians that goes deeper than skin color or ethnic background. We are the "body of Christ," which emphasizes the unity and necessity of each Christian for the well-being of the church. Because we are united in the most profound way, we are free to rejoice in our differences. We are free to see them not as sources of division, but as God meant them to be: sources of delight.

ENDNOTES

1. The Greek word translated as "reconciliation" is *katalasso*.
2. See especially 2 Corinthians 5:11–21; Romans 5:9–11; and Colossians 1:19–20.
3. Paul uses the Greek word *kosmos,* which is translated as "world"—thus a *cosmic* reconciliation.

4. This is what many theologians have called "objective justifi-cation." This teaching comes primarily from Romans 5:9–11, 2 Corinthians 5:11–21, and Colossians 1:19–20, passages which teach of the universal reconciliation of God in Christ. Thus, per-haps it would be preferable to refer to this comforting teaching as "universal or cosmic reconciliation" to better reflect the actual language of the Bible.

5. The Bible commonly speaks of God as having been grieved or hurt by sinful, human behavior (Genesis 6:6; Acts 5:3–4). God, after all, is a person and He has a personality. He takes our sins personally.

17

Peace

"Peace I leave with you; My peace I give you." (John 14:27)

ALL TORN UP INSIDE

Liu Feng needed help. She couldn't deny it any longer. It was starting to affect all her relationships. Her marriage had ended in divorce five years ago. Then she alienated her children, Joseph and Joy, both of whom had moved out within the past year. She hardly ever saw them anymore. Now she had succeeded in hurting her best friend, Carol. All Carol had suggested was that Liu get counseling. Carol was right. Liu knew that her life was coming apart at the seams. But she couldn't help herself. She felt all torn up inside.

Finally, Liu went to a Christian counselor who had been recommended by Carol's pastor. The counselor helped her come to grips with the divisions, the fractures, within herself. He helped her to see the cause of her psychological problems. They had to do with traumatic events that had occurred in her childhood, before she had come to America. He also read a passage from the Christian Bible to her. It was from John 14:27. Jesus tells His disciples: "Peace I leave with you; My peace I give you."

The words sounded strange yet intriguing to Lui. She did not know much about Christianity. She had been raised as a Buddhist, but she had not practiced any formal religion for more than 30 years. What could Jesus' promise of peace mean for her? She resolved to look into this further. She would talk to Carol. This could be just what she needed: peace for her troubled heart.

"My Peace I Give You"

Ultimately, *peace* is related to *reconciliation*. In fact, these two metaphors are so close that they cannot be separated. Rather, they identify two aspects of the same reality. *Reconciliation* emphasizes the condition of unity brought about by Christ's obedience while *peace* emphasizes the cessation of conflict that occurs at the same time. Despite this similarity, there is a distinction: *Reconciliation* signals the solution to the *separation* between people. *Peace* calls attention to the solution to the *friction* between and within people.

In the New Testament, *peace* draws on the rich meaning of the Hebrew concept of *shalom*. In the Old Testament, *shalom* is the general well-being God brings about for and in His people. He blesses His people with peace: "The Lord turn His face toward you and give you peace" (Numbers 6:26). He establishes His nation in peace (Psalm 29:11).

Peace also is a common and important aspect of the Old Testament's proclamation of the Gospel. It forms a significant part of the prophetic announcement of the Messiah. Isaiah prophesies: "I will extend peace to her like a river" (Isaiah 66:12). And Ezekiel foretells: "I will make a covenant of peace with them" (Ezekiel 37:26). In fact, sometimes the prophecy of peace is framed in personal terms. Micah declares: "And He will be their peace" (Micah 5:5). And Isaiah foretells of the one who will be called, "Wonderful Counselor, Mighty God, Everlasting Father, Prince of Peace" (Isaiah 9:6).

From this rich background, Jesus announces, "Peace I leave with you; My peace I give you. I do not give to you as the world gives. Do not let your hearts be troubled and do not be afraid" (John 14:27). Christ came to bring peace; He came to *be* peace for the world. He knew that His disciples would face conflict. He announced His assurance to them: "I have told you these things, so that in Me you may have peace. In this world you will have trouble. But take heart! I have overcome the world" (John 16:33). For a world marred by friction and conflict, Jesus is peace.

In the New Testament, *peace* is often personified. Jesus is called the "Lord of peace" (2 Thessalonians 3:16). In Ephesians 2:14, Paul writes: "For He Himself is our peace." Peace comes because of a person, and it comes in the form of a person. Peace is personified in Christ.

CONFLICT

Few maladies are more widely felt than the reality behind this *peace* metaphor. It is an inseparable element of our differences that they should be the occasion for conflict. We are a "conflicted" people, as evidenced by the fact that so many of our relationships are dysfunctional. Marriages are factious, friendships are antagonistic, and families are divided by feuds. There is conflict in our streets, in our workplace, in our home, and in our church. Disharmony is everywhere, and it affects all relations between people and between groups of people.

However, not all discord is external. Discord also affects people in their psyches as well. Many carry within them the seeds of friction. These seeds often go undetected. The fracture caused by an internal psychological breakdown often can be more painful and harmful than an open rupture between people. Internal torment can even cause the psyche to break into multiple personalities and other disorders that cripple individuals and cause the destruction of relationships. That's what happened to Liu. Her internal distress brought to ruin all her relationships and exacerbated her situation beyond her ability to bear it.

> For to us a Child is born, to us a Son is given, and the government will be on His shoulders. And He will be called Wonderful Counselor, Mighty God, Everlasting Father, Prince of Peace. (Isaiah 9:6)

What Liu didn't know was that her internal disunion was only a hint at a much greater and more vexing fissure between her and God. As her relationship problems were merely a window into a more serious internal breach, so her internal disconnection was but an image of her separation from God. All people have cut themselves off from God by their sin. We are a fractious people, bent on cutting ourselves off from the one who made us. We are unable to get along with one another, even with ourselves, because we can't get along with God. The real source of friction in our lives is our contention against God.

PEACE BEYOND ALL UNDERSTANDING

It's remarkable that Jesus has brought peace to this world, which He did, ironically, through a violent death. Jesus placed Himself in the breach. On the cross He was torn away from His Father. He suffered violence at the hand of an angry crowd. He endured internal peacelessness and agony on the Mount of Olives as He prayed, "Father, if You are willing, take this cup from Me; yet not My will, but Yours be done" (Luke 22:42). Jesus endured both external and internal conflict in our place. As a result, He brought about peace between us and our heavenly Father.

Yet there is a distinction between peace as a Gospel metaphor and the sense or feeling of peacefulness or contentment that Christians or non-Christians occasionally may experience. The peace that Christ is and brings is much more than our feeling or experience of tranquility. Jesus brings about the objective state of peace that transcends our experiences and is real despite our feelings to the contrary.

Christ's gift is like the declaration of peace between two warring parties. It is real and objective, even if some people don't feel particularly peaceful and continue to feel the effects of conflict. It is, as Paul says, a peace "which transcends all understanding" (Philippians 4:7). When we feel it, we rejoice in it as a gift from God. When we don't feel it, we rejoice that we are still, through Christ, at peace with God.

> Let the peace of Christ rule in your hearts, since as members of one body you were called to peace. And be thankful. Let the word of Christ dwell in you richly as you teach and admonish one another with all wisdom, and as you sing psalms, hymns and spiritual songs with gratitude in your hearts to God. And whatever you do, whether in word or deed, do it all in the name of the Lord Jesus, giving thanks to God the Father through Him. (Colossians 3:15–17)

God has not promised that all who have faith in Christ will be relieved of their internal and external friction. As in all other areas of life, Christians will be plagued by the ruptures, divisions, and conflicts that are part of life in this sinful world. However, in Christ, God has mended our most serious breach. The peace that exists between God and us does not depend on our perception or reflection of it. It is real and objective because Christ, our Prince of Peace, has made it real through His suffering on the cross. His death has opened the way for us to mend the fractures that plague our lives. Paul says it best: "Let the peace of Christ rule in your hearts, since as members of one body you were called to peace" (Colossians 3:15).

18

Forgiveness

"No longer will a man teach his neighbor, or a man his brother, saying, 'Know the LORD,' because they will all know Me, from the least of them to the greatest," declares the LORD. "For I will forgive their wickedness and will remember their sins no more." (Jeremiah 31:34)

FORGIVE AND FORGET?

"I'll never forget what you did," Becky told Abby. "I don't want to talk to you anymore. I hate you."

Becky couldn't forget the insult. First, Abby had flirted shamelessly with Jon, then she had laughed in her face and called her ugly. And Abby had done this in front of everyone.

Becky felt so ashamed and embarrassed, so hurt. It was even worse because last year, as freshmen, she and Abby had been best friends. Although Abby had later apologized, Becky couldn't bring herself to forgive her. Becky's friends told her to "forgive and forget," but she couldn't do it. She held the offense in her mind like a burning ember and refused to let go of it. Forgive and forget? How?

When Becky talked to her Dad about the incident, he showed her an interesting passage from the Old Testament.

Speaking through His prophet Jeremiah, God said to His people: "For I will forgive their wickedness and will remember their sins no more" (Jeremiah 31:34). The Israelites had been wicked. They had hurt and grieved their Lord terribly. For His own sake, though, God would forgive them. He simply would not remember their sins. He would put them out of His mind.

This made Becky think. When we sin against God, He gets angry and hurt, just like she was angry and hurt by Abby's actions. But God forgives *and* forgets. Can God, who knows everything, forget things? Becky couldn't imagine this. *If God really does forgive my sins against Him and forgets them,* Becky thought, *maybe I can forgive Abby and forget what she did too.*

I Will Remember Their Sins No More

Forgiveness is used several ways in Scripture. It is used as a commercial metaphor, denoting the cancellation of a debt. It also is used as a personal metaphor to illustrate what happens between people. *Forgiveness* is what happens when separation between people is resolved, when the occasion or cause of the division is eliminated or removed.[1] It is a common Gospel word in the Bible. In Scripture, the chasm between God and us that is caused by our sin is eliminated because of Christ's work in His active and passive obedience. Our sin is *forgiven*. It is removed as a cause of division between us and God. Forgiveness signals, therefore, the restoration of a wholesome relationship between God and His creatures. The way is now clear for the original relationship with God for which we were created.

Beyond this general meaning, however, *forgiveness* has unique features as a personal metaphor. First, forgiveness is commonly linked with repentance. At His ascension into heaven, Jesus said: "This is what is written: The Christ will suffer and rise from the dead on the third day, and repentance and forgiveness of sins will be preached in His name to all nations, beginning at Jerusalem" (Luke 24:46–47). Jesus identifies the central theme of the Gospel that He is entrusting to His disciples. Repentance, the acknowledgment of one's sinfulness and of one's sins, is a necessary prerequisite for forgiveness.

The apostle John writes: "If we confess our sins, He is faithful and just and will forgive us our sins" (1 John 1:9). The idea behind these ways of saying the Gospel is that the way to the restoration of a proper relationship is to acknowledge one's guilt and to confess it to the one against whom you have sinned. When we confess our sins to God, He forgives us, removing what separates us from Him. We are restored.[2]

A second unique feature to the *forgiveness* metaphor is that forgiveness is occasionally linked with forgetting, or at least with *not* remembering. Although less explicitly connected with the specific word *forgiveness,* Isaiah 43:25 says: "I, even I, am He who blots out your transgressions, for My own sake, and remembers your sins no more." Forgiving sins is said to be "remembering them no more." Even more colorfully, Isaiah 65:16–17 says: "For the past troubles will be forgotten and hidden from My eyes. Behold I will create new heavens and a new earth. The former things will not be remembered, nor will they come to mind."

The imagery is vivid and exciting. The God who always remembers His covenant with His people forgets. He who knows all things cannot and will not remember the sins He has forgiven. He simply hides them from His eyes. He does not let them come to mind. They are forgotten. He does not remember them. God "forgives and forgets."

> Who is a God like You, who pardons sin and forgives the transgression of the remnant of His inheritance? You do not stay angry forever but delight to show mercy. You will again have compassion on us; You will tread our sins underfoot and hurl all our iniquities into the depths of the sea. (Micah 7:18–19)

I JUST CAN'T FORGET

How different it is with us! When someone sins against us, we can't forget. We have eternal memories when it comes to the faults of others. Everyone can relate to this malady. We all have harbored grudges against those who have offended us. We are quick to take offense but slow to forgive. When it comes to the sins of others, our memories are perfect. A wife can remember every time her husband has looked at another woman. He can remember every time she has nagged him. A sister remembers every single time her big brother bullied her, while he remembers every time she got on his nerves. Our memories are better than any elephant when it comes to the wrongs of others.

When it comes to *our* sins, however, we suddenly develop total amnesia. We can't remember our own faults. Our forgetfulness about our own problems is complete. It is absolute. We don't want to admit we are wrong. We refuse to apologize, to confess, to repent. We go through life assuming that all our problems are caused by others. We are oblivious to our own failings. We simply can't remember them. This is the problem Becky had: She could not forget Abby's offense, and she could not remember her own faults and failures.

But our inability to forget the sins of others and to remember our own sins is merely symptomatic of a much deeper, more disturbing forgetfulness. We have forgotten that we are children of God and that we have sinned against Him "in thought, word, and deed." We have forgotten that we daily sin much and deserve nothing but God's wrath and punishment. We have forgotten that we have grieved our God, that we have hurt Him by our iniquity. We have a mental block, amnesia, utter forgetfulness about our trespasses. We have driven this from our minds. We have hidden it from our mind's eye. We have no recollection of it. We need to admit our wrong, confess it, and repent of it.

Divine Forgetfulness

When we admit our wrongs, confess them, and repent of them, our memories are miraculously refreshed and we are

154

reminded that God has remembered our plight. He has sent His only Son, Jesus Christ, to forgive us. God has not forgotten us. He has made an everlasting covenant with His people, which He will never forget. God's memory is perfect. He remembers the forgiving work of Jesus on the cross. He holds this before His mind's eye constantly, and He looks on us with the favor and love He has for us on account of Christ.

At the same time, and again miraculously, God forgets. He forgets our sins. He does not remember our trespasses. How remarkable is divine forgetfulness. God remembers only the goodness of Christ; He forgets our evil. He remembers the cross; He forgets our sin. God forgets in His remembering; He remembers in His forgetting. God's memory and God's forgetfulness have brought about the removal of our offense and have paved the way for us once again to be the people He originally created us to be: His people, His friends, His beloved children.

> For He has rescued us from the dominion of darkness and brought us into the kingdom of the Son He loves, in whom we have redemption, the forgiveness of sins. (Colossians 1:13–14)

Forgive and forget? We can because God has forgiven and forgotten our sins and will eternally remember His promises to us. In fact, God has given us the commission to forgive others as we have been forgiven. In John 20:23, Jesus tells His disciples: "If you forgive anyone his sins, they are forgiven; if you do not forgive them, they are not forgiven." It is not only possible for Christians to forgive those who sin against them, but it is a fundamental characteristic of Christians that they do so. Through faith in Christ, we are given the attitude of Christ (Philippians 2:5). Ever remembering God's forgiveness, we are ever forgetful of our neighbor's sins toward us.

ENDNOTES

1. It should be pointed out that *forgiveness* is, of all the metaphors, perhaps the most general in the sense that it has lost so much of

its metaphorical character. It is used often in Scripture in ways that may not readily be classifiable as commercial or personal. In fact, *forgiveness* is the most difficult Gospel word to classify. For example, a number of passages link forgiveness with healing (Psalm 103:3; Isaiah 33:24; Matthew 9:5–6). Still, there seems to be a firm enough pattern in the biblical use of this word to justify categorization according to the scheme presented in this book. This is a good place to once again remind ourselves of the fluidity of these metaphors and the freedom the biblical writers exhibited in their use.

2. It is worth pointing out that our repentance is never the "cause" of our forgiveness, as if God forgives us *because* we repent. The cause of our forgiveness is always in Scripture the forgiving work of Jesus Christ on the cross. So our repentance must not be thought of as a necessary prerequisite for forgiveness. Rather, our acknowledgment of sin and or sorrow over it breaks down the barrier to forgiveness that our lack of acknowledgment raises. A Christian always will give all glory to Christ for salvation and will never overemphasize personal repentance.

19

Marriage

"Go, proclaim this message toward the north: 'Return, faithless Israel,' declares the Lord, 'I will frown on you no longer, for I am merciful,' declares the Lord, 'I will not be angry forever. Only acknowledge your guilt—you have rebelled against the Lord your God, you have scattered your favors to foreign gods under every spreading tree, and have not obeyed Me,' declares the Lord. 'Return faithless people,' declares the Lord, 'for I am your husband. I will choose you—one from a town and two from a clan—and bring you to Zion.' " (Jeremiah 3:12–14)

DIVORCE

I'm leaving you, John, Karen wrote. That's all. She packed some things, took their daughter, and left the house. She would spend that night at her mother's. Beyond that, she was not sure what she would do, but she couldn't stay with John.

This was not the first time John had been unfaithful to her. The first time had been nearly 10 years ago, during their third year of marriage. John had been on a business trip. He had met whatever-her-name-was in the hotel bar. It had been a one-time thing. John had repented. Karen had forgiven him.

She had almost forgotten. As far as she knew, it had never happened again. Until now.

Her sense of indignation, even violation, was overpowering. John had violated his vows and her trust. He had allowed something destructive to come between them. Divorce was such an ugly word—so definitive, so final. What would she do? Where would she live? How would she support herself? What about Veronica, only 7 years old? It would devastate her. Karen's pain was almost unbearable. "How could he have done this?" she said repeatedly. She found herself hating him even as she remembered how much she had loved him on their wedding day.

At her mother's house, Karen attempted to make sense of what was happening. She and her mother read in Scripture: " 'Return, faithless people,' declares the LORD, 'for I am your husband' " (Jeremiah 3:14). That struck Karen. God's people in the Bible were like an unfaithful wife while God was like a faithful husband. That imagery hit home. Was she unfaithful to God? She hadn't given God much thought lately. Would God divorce her? She wondered if there was a connection between her marriage and her relationship with God.

"I AM YOUR HUSBAND"

One of the more intimate aspects of the personal metaphors is the cluster of images related to marriage. The imagery is framed in different ways—bridegroom and bride, wedding and wedding banquet, husband and wife—but the basic idea is that what happens as a result of the work of Christ is a new relationship with God that is similar to marriage. Because of Christ, God, our enemy because of our sin, becomes our husband. He woos us as a bridegroom does his bride. He marries us and makes us His beloved. He throws a great wedding banquet, a celebration of joy and union and faithfulness. He makes us His own, His bride.

Marriage is a rich metaphor in the Old Testament, one found in many beautiful passages. This metaphor is most vivid, however, in the book of the prophet Hosea. Hosea's entire life is a picture of God's love for His unfaithful people. The first three chapters of Hosea's book are autobiographical. He recounts his long-suffering love for his unfaithful wife, Gomer, and her obstinate, profligate unfaithfulness to him. She whores after other lovers while Hosea remains faithful and continues to love her and seek her. His marriage—tragic according to our standards—is a living prophecy, an enacted proclamation of God's love for us.

God loves His people even though they are unfaithful to Him. They chase after other gods, prostituting and selling themselves. But God remains faithful. Through Hosea, He calls His people back to Himself. God speaks the following remarkable words to His unfaithful, adulterous people:

> "Therefore I am now going to allure her; I will lead her into the desert and speak tenderly to her. ... In that day," declares the LORD, "you will call Me 'my husband'; you will no longer call Me 'my master.' ... I will betroth you to Me forever; I will betroth you in righteousness and justice, in love and compassion. I will betroth you in faithfulness, and you will acknowledge the LORD." (Hosea 2:14, 16, 19–20)[1]

The imagery is graphic. God woos His people back, wins us over with tender words. He marries us and promises to deal with us with righteousness, justice, love, compassion, and faithfulness. These are the components of a good marriage. These are the characteristics of God's actions toward us as husband.

Jesus also uses this theme, or variations of it, in His teachings in the New Testament. He tells several parables in which He compares the kingdom of heaven to a king who prepared a wedding banquet (Matthew 22:1–14; Luke 14:15–24) or to ten virgins who went to meet the bridegroom (Matthew 25:1–13; Luke 12:35–40). In Matthew 9:15, Jesus compares Himself to a bridegroom when asked by the Pharisees why His disciples don't fast. John the Baptist calls Jesus the bridegroom while he, John, is the attendant or "best man" (John 3:29).

> For your Maker is your husband—the LORD Almighty is His name—the Holy One of Israel is your Redeemer; He is called the God of all the earth. (Isaiah 54:5)

The other writers of the New Testament also made the connection between Jesus and a husband or bridegroom. Paul writes to the Corinthians: "I promised you to one husband, to Christ, so that I might present you as a pure virgin to Him" (2 Corinthians 11:2). In Ephesians 5:22–33, he also draws out the analogy between the husband/wife relationship and the relationship between Christ and the church. Finally, in an extravagant mixing of metaphors, John (in a vision) is introduced by one of the seven angels to "the bride, the wife of the Lamb" (Revelation 21:9).

UNFAITHFULNESS

It doesn't take much imagination to discover the malady behind the *marriage* metaphor. It is in the magazines, on the television, at the movies, in cheap paperback novels, everywhere illicit and promiscuous sex is celebrated—it is unfaithfulness or adultery. Our society tolerates, even embraces, marital infidelity. One of the few opinions on sex that is not tolerated in our liberated age is the one that promotes traditional values such as moderation, modesty, decency, and faithfulness.

Despite the appeal among the "cultural elite," casual attitudes toward sex have caused untold harm and destruction to human beings and their relationships. Divorce is rampant. Divided and blended families are the "norm." Marriage-for-life is regarded as old-fashioned. Adultery and its close cousin fornication are well on their way from vice to virtue.

To whatever extent they may be influenced by these factors, people know what malady lies behind the *marriage* metaphor. What people don't know, and what Karen didn't know at first, is that the rampant adultery of today is merely an image of a much more destructive adultery of which we are all guilty. Its name is different, but it sounds disturbingly similar: idolatry.

Like the Israelites of old, we are unfaithful to our God. In our own ways, we seek false gods and commit idolatry. We may not bow down to Baal, as Israel did, though false religiosity and false gods are making a comeback in our New Age search for meaning. We may not worship stone and wooden images, but we do commit idolatry every time we put our trust anywhere other than in God. When we trust our own merits or accomplishments, when we put our hope in the accumulation of wealth or in estate planning, when we love our material possessions and allow them to get in the way of our worship of the true God, then we commit idolatry. Martin Luther writes: "Where your heart is, there is your God."[2] We all are idolaters, all adulterers. We all are clamoring after self-gratification. If God gave us what we deserved, He would divorce us and separate us from His love and protection.

A Bride Beautifully Dressed

Thanks be to God! He loves us and does not divorce us. Instead, He woos us back. He sent His Son, Jesus Christ, to call us back to Himself so we might become His beloved bride. Although we are unfaithful to Him, God always remains faithful to us. We constantly fall, but He remains strong in His love for us.

> "For this reason a man will leave his father and mother and be united to his wife, and the two will become one flesh." This is a profound mystery—but I am talking about Christ and the church. (Ephesians 5:31–32)

His love wins us and keeps us and will not let us go. We can be sure: Nothing "will be able to separate us from the love of God that is in Christ Jesus our Lord" (Romans 8:39). But God has more to say. He genuinely rejoices in His marriage to us. That's the way the Bible presents it. Christ, the bridegroom, has great joy. He celebrates with parties and banquets. He invites the whole world to His wedding feast: "Let us rejoice and be glad and give Him glory! For the wedding of the Lamb has come, and His bride has made herself ready" (Revelation 19:7; see also Revelation 19:9).

Later, John envisions the bride as the church descending to the wedding to meet Christ, her husband: "I saw the Holy City, the new Jerusalem, coming down out of heaven from God, prepared as a bride beautifully dressed for her husband" (Revelation 21:2). What a lovely picture! The bride in her wedding dress comes to meet her bridegroom. He will love her, deal gently with her, and be faithful to her forever. What joy! What comfort! God will never divorce us, but He will love us always.

Of course, we are not always faithful to our God or to one another. When we are unfaithful to God, He forgives us and restores us as His beloved bride. When we are unfaithful to one another, we also are enabled to forgive one another because God has first loved us. The life of a Christian is not necessarily a life of "marital bliss" and happiness. We all are sinners. But God has taken us as His bride. He enables us to be faithful to one another and to forgive one another.

ENDNOTES

1. The latter part of this passage is significant also because of the important theological terminology it contains. *Righteousness* (*tzdak*) is a major theme in the Old Testament (as well as in the New) that emphasizes God's declaration of sinners as righteous for His own sake. (See Genesis 15:6.) It is also the basis for the legal metaphors of the Gospel. See part 4 for more information. *Justice* (*mishpat*), also a major theological category, emphasizes God's establishment of justice on the earth. *Love* (*chesed*) is that virtually untranslatable word for which Hosea is especially noted. It means grace, love, devotion, loving-kindness, etc. *Compassion* (*racham*) is yet another Hebrew word for "grace" or "love," often with the connotation of compassion or mercy. *Faithfulness* (*amunah*) conveys the idea that God can be counted on to act with integrity. Finally, *acknowledgment* (*yadah*) has to do with the intimate knowledge, or faith, whereby one "knows"

another in a most personal way. All of these words describe the "ideal" relationship between God and man, mirroring God's posture toward us. Please note also that they serve as an excellent summary of the qualities that would make for an excellent marriage.

2. "The Large Catechism," in *The Book of Concord* (ed. Theodore G. Tappert; Philadelphia: Fortress Press, 1959), 365.

PART 6

CHRIST THE PRIEST, CHRIST THE LAMB: SACRIFICIAL METAPHORS

20

Expiation/Priestly Mediation

For this reason He had to be made like His brothers in every way, in order that He might become a merciful and faithful high priest in service to God, and that He might make atonement for the sins of the people. Because He Himself suffered when He was tempted, He is able to help those who are being tempted. (Hebrews 2:17–18)

A Fearsome God

Juanita was afraid of God. She always had been afraid of Him. She believed in God, but she didn't like Him very much. That's why she hadn't been to church since she'd been married. It didn't help that her husband, Mario, wanted nothing to do with the church. But Juanita didn't go because she didn't want to. God seemed so distant, so fearsome. It seemed that He always was angry and unapproachable. She prayed, but He did not seem to hear. She told Him all her problems, but He didn't seem to care.

Going to church only made things more difficult for Juanita. There she heard stories about how angry God was because of her sins. It seemed He always was bringing judgment on people, always condemning them. She thought it would be better to stay away from church. Maybe that way she would not have to think about God. But not going to church made her feel more guilty, which only increased her fear of God. Why did God have to be that way? Why couldn't He be more loving and tender?

One day Juanita's friend Maria invited her to a Bible study at a different church. Although she was skeptical, Juanita agreed to go. What she heard there struck at the heart of her fear of God. The leader read from the book of Hebrews: "For this reason [Jesus] had to be made like His brothers in every way, in order that He might become a merciful and faithful high priest in service to God, and that He might make atonement for the sins of the people"(2:17).

Juanita thought, *Jesus is like us in every way? Isn't He God? Does God really know what it's like to be human? Is Jesus really a "merciful high priest" who comes between God's anger and my sin, turning God's wrath away so I can be forgiven?* "I should rethink my conception of who God is," Juanita told Maria. "Maybe He's not so fearsome after all."

A MERCIFUL AND FAITHFUL HIGH PRIEST

The sacrificial metaphors for the Gospel are among the most common Gospel metaphors in Scripture. Sacrifice was so much a part of the lives and experience of God's Old Testament believers that sacrificial imagery and themes are reflected on nearly every page of the Bible. What the New Testament has to say about the work of Christ on our behalf is often linked with the provision of salvation God gave through the sacrificial system.

Using sacrificial metaphors today, however, raises more questions than answers. For most people in the western world, the notions of appeasement, blood, and slaughter of animals are foreign and unappealing. Thoughts of sacrifices evoke a world of unpleasant, even repugnant, associations. Sprinkling blood on people seems barbaric. We are repulsed by these things, and we try, as much as possible, to confine death and bleeding to hospitals. In many respects, therefore, the biblical world is a foreign world, one that is beyond the experience of most people in western societies.

Another reason why sacrificial metaphors are difficult for modern people to grasp is the conception of God that lies behind these ways of saying the Gospel. Perhaps more than any other metaphor, *sacrifice* is predicated on the fact that God is angry at humanity's sin and that His wrath requires appeasement. This idea, though thoroughly biblical, is repulsive to most people today. Rather than thinking of God as an angry, fearsome God to whom we must sacrifice something, or someone, most people think of God as a kindly or even doting father-figure. People are more comfortable with God as "friend" or "brother" or a "white-haired grandfatherly man" than with the wrathful God of Scripture.[1]

At the same time, the malady underlying *sacrifice* and *appeasement* is powerfully felt by people, even if they don't specifically connect their experiences with the sacrificial context. We know fear. We sense our incompleteness. We feel that we are, in some way, flawed. We recognize that we are filthy and unclean. Life today certainly is filled with fear and frustration. Although many people may not appreciate the metaphors at first glance, they are relevant to our condition.

We cannot do justice to the depth and richness of the primary "means of grace" God provided to His Old Testament believers from Moses to Christ. We will, however, get a flavor of the sacrificial metaphors so the biblical witness (not only of the Old Testament!) can be restored to the Christian proclamation of the Gospel. The sacrificial system of the Old Testament embraced the full experience and life of God's ancient people. The metaphor can speak today, too, and take its rightful place in the proclamation of the Gospel.[2]

A primary aspect of sacrificial metaphors in Scripture is that Jesus is *expiation* or *propitiation* for the sins of the people.[3] *Expiation* and *propitiation* often are used interchangeably as synonyms. However, they are different, just as two sides of a coin are different. While the meaning of both words is somewhat fluid, *expiation* generally refers to the guilt of the sin that is taken away. *Propitiation* refers generally to the idea that, through the sacrifice, God's wrath is satisfied. In other words, when we say our sin is *expiated,* we mean that its significance before God is eliminated. When we say that God is *propitiated,* we mean that He is no longer angry because of our sin. In either case, sin, the cause of our offense to God, is removed.

In the Old Testament, this removal occurred through sacrifices, through the shedding of the blood of an "innocent one," one without guilt or stain or blemish. The blood, which in the Hebraic way of thinking contained the essence of life (Leviticus 17:11), "covered up" the sins of the people or "washed" their sins away.[4] Thus, as the blood was shed, God's wrath was propitiated, the sins of the people were expiated, bringing about atonement.

> Because on this day atonement will be made for you, to cleanse you. Then, before the LORD, you will be clean from all your sins. It is a sabbath of rest, and you must deny yourselves; it is a lasting ordinance. The priest who is anointed and ordained to succeed his father as high priest is to make atonement. He is to put on the sacred linen garments and make atonement for the Most Holy Place, for the Tent of Meeting and the altar, and for the priests and all the people of the community. (Leviticus 16:30–33)

Behind this imagery is the strong picture of the God who is wrathful because of the sins of the people. His wrath will not simply disappear or be set aside. Something must appease Him. Something must wash away our guilt or hide it from God so the separation, the hurt brought about in God because of sin, might be turned away. There is no way to get around this aspect of the biblical understanding of God, as unpleasant or unappealing as it may be. He is angry because of sin. He is a "jealous God," a wrathful God, who will vent His anger if nothing is done to restore Him to a favorable disposition toward us.

However, God is not like the pagan gods who are arbitrary in their response to human appeasement. God Himself has provided the means by which humans may regain His favor. It is not as though we were "buying" God's favor. The God of Israel cannot be bought. Rather, He has given the people a means of averting His wrath. In fact, as Hebrews 2:17 suggests, God Himself provides the atonement. In the Old Testament, God did it by providing priests and sacrifices as means of expiation. In the Gospel, however, we see that the propitiation is made by Jesus, our high priest. God performs all the functions in expiating our guilt: Jesus is the priest, the one making atonement. Thus, He takes away the sins of the world.

Jesus accomplished this expiation by being "made like His brothers in every way" (Hebrews 2:17). An important aspect of the sacrificial system is that one must serve as a substitute for the guilty: The lamb without blemish is a substitute for the sinful people. The scapegoat dies in the place of the people. Christ was our substitute. He died on the altar of the cross, shedding His blood so we wouldn't have to, dying sacrificially so we would not have to. Christ played the roles—sacrifice and priest—substituting for us and bringing about the propitiation of God.

SINNERS IN THE HANDS OF AN ANGRY GOD

Jonathan Edwards' well-known treatise *Sinners in the Hands of an Angry God* defined a period of United States' history. The theological problem of the 18th century was perceived to be that God was angry. The greatest need for humans was to appease God's wrath. Edwards' treatise makes for interesting reading, particularly for its historical value, because rarely do people care whether God is angry. In fact, most people reject the notion that God is wrathful, preferring instead to view God as loving and gentle. Modern people don't know *God* as angry, but *we* sure are angry.

Anger is everywhere. Parents are angry with their children. Children are angry with their parents. Students are angry with their teachers and teachers with their students. Spouses are angry with each other. Rage is all the rage today. Road rage, gender rage, age rage—anger is apparent at every turn. Why can't we accept the notion that God would be enraged at us because of our sin? Perhaps it's because we have forgotten the idea of righteous rage, just anger. Most of our anger arises from our sinfulness—our impatience or disrespect or inconsiderateness with one another. Anger causes damage, an offense between individuals that is hard to cover over.

God is angry without being sinful. In His anger, He is like a father who is wronged by his child. The father is rightly angered, justly wrathful, at the disobedience of his child. He is right to punish the child, though he does it not out of anger, but as an attempt to make the child turn from disobedience and be restored to favor. In the same way, God's anger and punishment are fundamentally different from the rage we see all around us. God's anger is for the good of people. Its objective is to restore, not to destroy; to heal, not to hurt. God's anger is different from sinful human anger, but He is still angry. His anger needs to be turned aside.

The anger we experience in our lives is a sinful, distorted image of a much more profound rage that God has because of our sins. God is offended by our sin, and He cannot "sweep it under the rug." He can't just "forget about it." Something must be done to appease God, to restore His offended honor, to compensate Him for His injury. That's what Juanita sensed, even though only intuitively. She sensed that God really was angry with her and that she was helpless to do anything about it. All of her efforts to please God through her own efforts only made her feel more guilty and made God more angry. She couldn't do it herself.

GUILT COVERING

Thank God, Juanita doesn't have to do it herself. God has already done it for her. Paul writes: "God presented Him [Jesus] as a sacrifice of atonement, through faith in His blood" (Romans 3:25).

Jesus is the "guilt-covering." He is the "Lamb of God" (John 1:36). His blood was shed so we could live. He was our substitute, dying for us on the cross so we might see God not as angry and wrathful, but as loving and kind. True, God was angry with us, but He is not angry anymore. Our guilt has been expiated. God has been propitiated.

The work of Christ is universal. The author of the epistle to the Hebrews writes: "So Christ was sacrificed once to take away the sins of many people" (Hebrews 9:28). St. John writes that Jesus Christ "is the atoning sacrifice for our sins, and not only for ours but also for the sins of the whole world" (1 John 2:2). God's wrath has been turned away from the entire world because of Christ's sacrifice. Although He was angry with the entire fallen world, God now favors all creation with His love and forgiveness. He is fully satisfied with Christ's sacrifice. It is "once for all" (Hebrews 10:10), putting an end to the need for further sacrifices and further propitiation. God is satisfied. Christ's sacrifice is enough.

Jesus satisfied His heavenly Father by becoming not only the sacrificial victim, but also the priest. He has mediated for us, placing Himself between us and the angry God. He has offered sacrifices on our behalf. He is our "merciful and faithful high priest" (Hebrews 2:17), according to the "order of Melchizedek" (Psalm 110:4). In a bit of a metaphorical stretch, Jesus assumes all the roles. He performs the sacrifice; He is sacrificed. We are atoned. Through His high priestly service, we are made priests. St. Peter writes: "You also, like living stones, are being built into a spiritual house to be a holy priesthood, offering spiritual sacrifices acceptable to God through Jesus Christ" (1 Peter 2:5).

173

What an incredible and unexpected ending! Rather than cringing in fear before a holy God who rages at us because of our sinful disobedience, we are loved, forgiven, and called priests. Although every person has direct access to God through faith in Christ and no longer needs intermediaries such as priests, God deigns to call us priests and invites us to serve as intermediaries for those who do not yet know Him as the loving and gentle Father we know Him to be through faith in Christ. What a blessing! We are priests, declaring to others "the praises of Him who called [us] out of darkness into His wonderful light" (1 Peter 2:9).

ENDNOTES

1. The depiction of God as wrathful in the Old Testament as opposed to the New Testament has caused some people wrongly to think of the God of the Old Testament as the "God of the Law," or the "God of wrath," and the God of the New Testament as the "God of love or grace." Of course, nothing could be further from the truth. It is the same God, the God of the Law and of the Gospel, who is found in both testaments. The sacrificial system of the Old Testament was a gracious gift from God whereby He provided His people with the opportunity to enjoy His love and favor.

2. To speak of the sacrifice of Christ as a "metaphor" requires some clarification. Although the New Testament writers, under the inspiration of the Holy Spirit, interpreted the work of Christ as the fulfillment of the sacrificial system of the Old Testament, Jesus was not, strictly speaking, a "sacrifice." He was not a "lamb," He was not a "priest." His blood was not shed on an "altar." Of course, He really did die on a cross, and there He really did shed His blood. And, of course, the sacrifices of the Old Testament were efficacious means of grace before God. But the juxtaposition of the two—the death of Jesus on a cross and the death of a lamb on an altar—is metaphorical. To speak of the implications of the fact of Jesus' death, the biblical writers "borrowed" from the realm of the sacrificial, thus speaking metaphorically.

3. The Greek words *hilasterion* and *exilasmos* can be translated as *expiation* or *propitiation*. The NIV translates *hilasterion* as "sacrifice of atonement" (Romans 3:25).

4. The "mercy seat" (NRSV) or "atonement cover" (NIV) of the ark in the tabernacle was the place where the blood was sprinkled and thus covered the sins of the people so the Lord did not see them anymore. See Exodus 25–26 and Leviticus 16.

21

Sacrificial Lamb

We all, like sheep, have gone astray, each of us has turned to his own way; and the Lord has laid on Him the iniquity of us all. He was oppressed and afflicted, yet He did not open His mouth; He was led like a lamb to the slaughter, and as a sheep before her shearers is silent, so He did not open His mouth. (Isaiah 53:6–7)

No Beauty

"How could you do this to yourself, Angel?"

Angel's parents, John and Elaine, simply couldn't understand what had led up to this situation. Their daughter was in the ICU. She had almost died. John and Elaine didn't understand why Angel, a beautiful 17-year-old, would starve herself nearly to death.

John and Elaine felt they should have noticed what was happening. Angel confessed that the past few months had been a blur of bingeing and purging, which she had kept from them until the past few weeks. Her bulimia had almost killed her. Angel said she hated her body. Even when she fell below 100 pounds, she said she felt fat and ugly.

Angel said her imperfections were always on her mind, waking and sleeping. She eventually became so emaciated, so sickly, that she seemed to be a different person. And the shame she had felt kept her from telling her parents or her friends. She had been unable to ask for help. She said she believed everyone thought of her the way she thought about herself. She imagined that everyone was disgusted by her appearance.

In the hospital, with tubes and needles providing much-needed nourishment to her starved body, John and Elaine sat by Angel's side. John read to his daughter a Bible passage he recently had heard at church. It was from the book of Isaiah:

> He grew up before Him like a tender shoot, and like a root out of dry ground. He had no beauty or majesty to attract us to Him, nothing in His appearance that we should desire Him. He was despised and rejected by men, a man of sorrows, and familiar with sufferings. Like one from whom men hide their faces He was despised, and we esteemed Him not. Surely He took up our infirmities and carried our sorrows, yet we considered Him stricken by God, smitten by Him, and afflicted. But He was pierced for our transgressions, He was crushed for our iniquities; the punishment that brought us peace was upon Him, and by His wounds we are healed. (Isaiah 53:2–5)

John remembered that this passage was speaking of the Servant of the Lord. He told Angel that Isaiah was speaking about Jesus. People were appalled at Jesus because He, too, was disfigured. People wanted to hide their faces from Him as He gave His life on the cross.

This concept made Angel think. Was Jesus like her? Did people find Him disgusting as He suffered for their sins? Was His appearance also so disfigured that they turned away from Him, as she imagined people were doing with her? Such insights made Angel begin to think a little differently about herself. If Jesus would do this for her, maybe she could learn to accept herself and be more satisfied with her body.

A Lamb without Blemish

Jesus is the "guilt-offering" who atoned for the sins of the world, expiating our sins and propitiating God. He shed His blood, covering over the sins of all people. In His sacrifice, Jesus, the Son of God, took on Himself our imperfections and gave us His flawlessness. Because Jesus is sinless, He fulfilled the Law perfectly as only He could. In Scripture, Christ's perfection is often phrased as the perfect lamb,[1] the one without blemish, whose shed blood covers the flaws and imperfections of God's sinful creatures. Thus, as *sacrificial lamb,* Jesus' perfection takes the place of our imperfections.

> The next day John saw Jesus coming toward him and said, "Look, the Lamb of God, who takes away the sin of the world!" (John 1:29)

The New Testament writers interpret Jesus as the fulfillment, the completion, of the Old Testament system of sacrifices. Masterfully mixing his metaphors, St. Peter writes: "For you know that it was not with perishable things such as silver or gold that you were redeemed from the empty way of life handed down to you from your forefathers, but with the precious blood of Christ, a lamb without blemish or defect" (1 Peter 1:18–19). He begins with the commercial metaphor of *redemption* and paying a price, but he concludes with the imagery of Christ as the perfect lamb, the one without blemish or defect, who would satisfy God's demand for perfection. Previously, Peter had reminded his readers that they were to be perfect: "But just as He who called you is holy, so be holy in all you do; for it is written: 'Be holy, because I am holy' " (1 Peter 1:15–16). Although we were not holy—on our own we could not be—Christ, "the one without blemish or defect," was holy for us. Through Him, we come into full perfection. Christ's perfection is ours, just as the perfection of the lamb to be sacrificed substituted for the imperfections of the people.

DISFIGURED

The malady behind this *sacrificial lamb* metaphor is obvious. We are flawed and disfigured, lacking the perfection and integrity that God demands. Of course, not all of us hold as deeply the perception of being "blemished" as Angel did. But all of us are flawed. Our imperfection is always before us. Dissatisfaction with ourselves—our physical, emotional, psychological, and economic selves—may well be the most common experience of life today. Although it may be phrased in a million ways, people are keenly aware of their deficiencies. How often have we thought or said, "I don't like my nose, my thighs, my legs"? Billions of dollars are spent in the United States on creams to smooth out wrinkles, on pills or programs to control weight, on surgeries to lift and tuck the effects of gravity, on vitamins to delay the impact of aging, on clothes that "slim us down," or on lotions to thicken thinning hair. We are a society that is more than aware of its imperfections, even imperfections that seem trivial. We are tuned in to our imperfections. The pursuit of the perfect body seems to be a national pastime.

What we don't know, however, is that our imperfections—even minor ones—are only a hint of a much deeper imperfection that we all have before God because of our sins. God is holy, and He demands holiness from all His creatures. But we are not holy. We are not perfect. We are flawed not only in our bodies and psyches, not only in our relationships with others, but in our most fundamental relationship—our relationship with God. God turns His face away from us in horror at our blemishes and imperfections. We are repugnant to Him. He is repulsed by us. God will not have anything to do with us.

PERFECT FOREVER

But there is a substitute for us. Christ became imperfect for us. The lamb without blemish became "like one from whom men hide their faces" (Isaiah 53:3). He took on Himself all our imperfections, all our blemishes, and all our flaws. He was "led like a lamb to the slaughter.... He was cut off from the land of the living, for the transgression of My people He was stricken" (Isaiah 53:7–8). As Jesus hung on the cross and bore the sins of the world, God turned His face from His only Son. He turned in horror from His beloved one. He abandoned His Son on the cross because He was bearing the unholiness of all people.

The Son of God has made us *perfect.* "By one sacrifice He has made perfect forever those who are being made holy" (Hebrews 10:14). Perfect forever! What wonderful news. There still may be much about us that we do not like, that we think of as less than perfect. But there is nothing about us that God doesn't like, nothing that is less than perfect in His eyes. Christ has been our substitute, taking our imperfections on Himself and through faith giving us His perfection, His fullness, and His integrity. What joy this gives us! We can live "satisfied" with ourselves because God is satisfied with us for Christ's sake.

> Then I heard every creature in heaven and on earth and under the earth and on the sea, and all that is in them, singing: "To Him who sits on the throne and to the Lamb be praise and honor and glory and power, for ever and ever!" (Revelation 5:13)

This doesn't mean that we now enjoy full and visible perfection. We still live in the time of faith. Our perfection is visible to us only through faith, not yet by sight. We will continue to experience the limitations of our flawed and sinful life. Only on the last day will we enjoy the visible and uninterrupted perfection won for us by Christ. Meanwhile, we are able by faith to see through to the end of our imperfections and to that day when all our weaknesses will be eliminated and we will rejoice in the perfection of our Father's heavenly kingdom.

At that time, we will join the angelic hosts in praising God and saying: "Worthy is the Lamb, who was slain, to receive power and wealth and wisdom and strength and honor and glory and praise!" (Revelation 5:12). And in that day, ironically and wonderfully, all who now suffer disgrace and shame will know that "the Lamb at the center of the throne will be their shepherd; He will lead them to springs of living water. And God will wipe away every tear from their eyes" (Revelation 7:17).

ENDNOTE

1. The imagery associated with sheep and shepherds is powerful and common in Scripture. However, there is a difference between Jesus as shepherd and Jesus as sacrificial lamb. As shepherd, Jesus is protector and guide and provider while we are the sheep. This imagery has little to do with sacrifices. Thus, while it is on the surface similar and in its own right quite interesting, it must be treated as a distinct metaphor. It also may be helpful at this point to make clear why the popular metaphor of Jesus as Good Shepherd is not used in this book as a Gospel metaphor. The reason is that the shepherd/sheep imagery is not generally associated with what Jesus did to solve our problem with God. Rather, it has to do with Christ's relationship to those who already are God's own. Thus, while *shepherd* may not be an appropriate justification metaphor, it is an excellent sanctification metaphor.

22

Hallowing/Cleansing

Husbands, love your wives, just as Christ loved the church and gave Himself up for her to make her holy, cleansing her by the washing with water through the word, and to present her to Himself as a radiant church, without stain or wrinkle or any other blemish, but holy and blameless. (Ephesians 5:25–27)

I Feel So Dirty

"How could God love me?" Claudia asked. "I feel so dirty." Ever since the rape, Claudia had an overwhelming sense of shame, of unworthiness. She felt unclean.

In her mind, Claudia knew better. The rape wasn't her fault. She had tried to be aware of her surroundings, careful not to go to the wrong places at the wrong times. But it had happened when she least expected it—at the mall in broad daylight. It made her sick to think about it, even now, months later. The shameful feelings would come over her at the strangest times—in a restaurant, at night in bed, but especially at the mall. She knew her attacker had been caught and was awaiting trial. She knew it was his fault. So why did she feel so filthy?

Claudia remembered trying to wash the stain of the attack away, the long showers many times a day. But she could not get clean. She felt that others looked at her as unclean, too, and avoided her. They said it was just that they were uncomfortable with her pain and never knew what to say or do around her. Claudia, "knew," however, that she was tainted and that they wanted to keep her at a distance. Her friends drifted away. Her husband felt abandoned, and their relationship was slipping away. She was having trouble with life, even with God.

Her counselor, Janet, was helping Claudia deal with her feelings of shame and disgrace and come to grips with the evil that had happened to her. But Janet also cared deeply about Claudia's relationship with God. She shared a Bible passage with Claudia that seemed to speak to her in clear and comforting tones: "Christ loved the church and gave Himself up for her to make her holy, cleansing her by the washing with water through the word " (Ephesians 5:25).

Could it be that, on account of the washing of my Baptism, I am without stain or wrinkle, holy and blameless before God? Claudia thought. *Could it be that God loved me after all?* If God could overlook her feelings of uncleanness and shame, maybe Claudia could do so as well.

A Fragrant Offering and Sacrifice to God

A final aspect of the sacrificial metaphors is *cleansing* or *hallowing*. Sacrifices expiate the guilt of sin through the shedding of blood, thus propitiating God's wrath. An important part of the sacrifices was the substitution of a perfect lamb for the imperfections and flaws of the people and the consequent bestowal of perfection and wholeness on the people.[1] Through the sacrifices, God's people were also *cleansed*[2] or *hallowed*[3]. They were made pure so they could stand in the presence of the holy God.

Cleansing is a tremendously rich concept in Scripture, especially in the Old Testament. In the biblical world, people became unclean before God in many ways. Certain foods, particularly bloody or rotten foods, were unclean. Infectious skin diseases, such as leprosy, could cause a person to become unclean. Mildew could render cloths or woolens unclean. In addition, a woman was considered to be unclean during and for a time after menstruating and for a period of time following childbirth. For all these situations, God prescribed procedures for restoring a person or a thing to its clean state.

Despite the great detail and, at times, strange procedures outlined in Scripture, what lies behind this aspect of the sacrificial system is quite simple to understand. God is holy. He is free of any corruption or filth. He cannot and will not allow Himself to become tainted by the stain of sin. Before He receives people into His presence, before He favors human beings with His grace, we must be purged of all offenses that pollute us and cause God to recoil from us. All these things—indeed, all human sin—are a stench and a foul smell before God.

God graciously provided a system whereby His people could be cleansed and thus enjoy His presence. All the sacrifices of the Old Testament find their fulfillment in Jesus. Paul writes: "Christ loved us and gave Himself up for us as a fragrant offering and sacrifice to God" (Ephesians 5:2). Christ is the end of all the sacrifices. He cleanses us from the pollution of our sin and enables God to love us and favor us with His presence. He presents us to Himself "without stain or wrinkle or any other blemish, but holy and blameless" (Ephesians 5:27).[4]

> Have mercy on me, O God, according to Your unfailing love; according to Your great compassion blot out my transgressions. Wash away all my iniquity and cleanse me from my sin. (Psalm 51:1–2)

DEFILED

We all relate to defilement. We "get our hands dirty" through our participation in some nefarious scheme. We are offended by rotten or spoiled food, especially meat. Many people are afraid of, or at least queasy about, blood. We turn away from unclean things, such as skin diseases and putrefaction.

We are increasingly aware of the negative effects of pollution on our environment, including oil spills, deforestation, or the destruction of plant and animal habitats. We are all familiar with dirt and filth.

All this is only a window on a more profound and troubling uncleanness that affects us all. Before God, all people are unclean, tainted, polluted. God is holy, and our filthiness is a personal offense to Him. We never will have access to Him, He will never come near us, as long as we remain contaminated. Try as we might, we cannot purify ourselves. God declares, "Although you wash yourself with soda and use an abundance of soap, the stain of your guilt is still before Me" (Jeremiah 2:22).

You Have Been Brought Near

But God does come near because Jesus has come near. He entered into our defiled existence, and through His blood we have been cleansed. Our prayer is: "Wash away all my iniquity and cleanse me from my sin. ... Cleanse me with hyssop, and I will be clean; wash me, and I will be whiter than snow" (Psalm 51:2, 7). God answered our prayer by sending His only Son. Therefore, God does not recoil from us in horror, but He comes near to us, favoring us with His presence. St. Paul says this in a particularly meaningful way: "But now in Christ Jesus you who once were far away have been brought near through the blood of Christ" (Ephesians 2:13).

God is not afraid to make His dwelling with us, as in His temple (1 Corinthians 3:16). We have been fully purified, as St. John writes: "The blood of Jesus, His Son, purifies us from all sin" (1 John 1:7). The cleansing blood of Jesus on the cross is applied in the purifying effects of Baptism. We often say Baptism is washes away our sins. St. Paul says in Titus 3:5: "He saved us through the washing of rebirth and renewal by the Holy Spirit." Baptism is a washing, which renews and purifies us before God. Instead of the blood of lambs and goats, the blood of Christ cleanses us (Hebrews 9:13–14).

Baptism is a source of great comfort to us, particularly when we feel filthy. When we feel unworthy of God, our Baptism reminds us that God has come near to us. We can, therefore, approach Him without fear (Hebrews 10:22). He has spoken to us by name, claiming us, cleansing us, and putting the saving mark of the cross on our head and on our heart. When we feel unclean, Paul's words are a sure comfort: "But you were washed, you were sanctified, you were justified in the name of the Lord Jesus Christ and by the Spirit of our God" (1 Corinthians 6:11).

ENDNOTES

1. Not all Old Testament sacrifices were lambs. A perfect specimen of any "clean" animal—for example, a dove or cow—could be offered. Even the "firstfruits," the best of the land's produce, was acceptable to God.

2. The Greek word translated as "cleansed" is *katharos*.

3. The Greek word translated as "hallowed" is *agios*, which generally means "to be made holy or sanctified."

4. It is important to make a clear distinction between the use of the word *hallow* or *sanctify* in Scripture as a Gospel metaphor and its use in Scripture and in theological writings to refer to what results from the Gospel. Sometimes the word is used to denote what God does *for* us in Christ: Christ cleanses us and makes us holy before God so we can come into His presence. At other times, the word is used to denote what Christ does *in* us, that is, what results from the Gospel, namely our sanctification, growth, and maturation in the "holiness" God has given us as we continue doing good works that are pleasing to God. Basically, this is the distinction common in theological works between *justification* and *sanctification*. The point to be remembered here, however, is that *sanctification* terminology is often used in Scripture to refer to *justification*.

PART 7

CHRIST THE SAVIOR:
DELIVERANCE METAPHORS

23

Salvation

Find rest, O my soul, in God alone; my hope comes from Him. He alone is my rock and my salvation; He is my fortress, I will not be shaken. My salvation and my honor depend on God; he is my mighty rock, my refuge. Trust in Him at all times, O people; pour out your hearts to Him, for God is our refuge. (Psalm 62:5–8)

ON THE BRINK OF DISASTER

"It's a war out there," Sergeant Smally said, "so be careful!" Frank Billings barely heard him. He was deep in his own thoughts. It was his first day back after the incident.

Incident sounded so insignificant. In reality, it was the most important *incident* of Frank's 28 years on the force. For almost three decades, he had stared danger in the face without so much as blinking. Then came the *incident*.

It had been a routine domestic disturbance call—a husband getting violent with his wife. Frank had handled dozens of cases like it. This time, however, as he and his partner were subduing the man, he came up with a pistol and fired four shots before Frank could wrestle it from his hand. Frank had felt one bullet whiz past his ear.

It wasn't until after he had secured the man that he realized his partner, Ozzie, had taken a bullet. It was only a flesh wound, but it was enough to put Ozzie out for a couple of weeks. It had really scared Frank. Forty-eight years old and only two years away from retirement, Frank was confronted with his own mortality. Now, on his first day back after 30 days on administrative leave, Frank wasn't sure he could handle the fear. It *was* a war out there. There were hidden dangers on all sides. He felt as though he were on the brink of disaster.

Just that morning, Frank's wife, Loretta, had read him a psalm from Scripture. She knew how anxious he was about returning to the precinct. She said this psalm was one she read each day when she felt worried about Frank. She read: "My soul finds rest in God alone; my salvation comes from Him. He alone is my rock and my salvation; He is my fortress, I will never be shaken" (Psalm 62:1–2).

Never had a Bible passage seemed so meaningful to Frank. Never had one spoken so directly to his needs. God would snatch him from danger and would be his strength and protection. God would save him from danger.

MY ROCK AND MY SALVATION

In Scripture, *salvation* often has the connotation of restoring a person to good health. *Salvation* also is used, however, in the sense of snatching someone from peril. It denotes deliverance from danger or removal of a person from a life-threatening situation. *Salvation* can mean "keeping someone alive" or "benefiting someone," as in restoring someone's well-being or preserving a person's "inner being" or inner health. Primarily, though, *salvation* is related to the context of danger, warfare, and chaos. To save a person is to rescue him or her from threatening circumstances and potential destruction.

Salvation is one of the least alive metaphors in Scripture. Because of its common and diffuse usage, its metaphorical value rarely is appreciated by Bible readers. It is the most generic Gospel term. *Salvation* often is used in a way that implies one of its derivative connotations (such as "keeping," "benefiting," "preserving," etc.) with the result that the word loses its picture-evoking power. As a result, much of its interesting and dynamic quality is lost. The person who wishes to communicate this metaphor with clarity and vigor will need a great deal of creativity. When used effectively, however, *salvation* is a vivid and exciting Gospel word.

The original connotation, and consequently the vividness, of this word perhaps can best be seen in its Old Testament usage.[1] The idea of snatching one from danger or peril is evident in the references to the salvation of Yahweh. Isaiah writes: "The LORD will lay bare His holy arm in the sight of all the nations, and all the ends of the earth will see the salvation of our God" (Isaiah 52:10). The psalmist exclaims: "Sing to the LORD a new song, for He has done marvelous things; His right hand and His holy arm have worked salvation for Him" (Psalm 98:1). The picture is quite graphic: God reaches out His strong arm and snatches us from the precipice. He pulls us back from the brink of disaster and saves us.

Another vivid image in the Old Testament that is related to *salvation* is the metaphor of God as a *rock* or a *sure foundation.* Such language contributes to the strength and vitality of the Gospel. The psalmist exalts: "My soul finds rest in God alone; my salvation comes from Him. He is my rock and my salvation; He is my fortress, I will never be shaken" (Psalm 62:1–2). Salvation is like God providing a solid place on which to stand in a world crumbling around us or like God's provision of a fortress in which to seek refuge from enemies who pursue us. At times God is likened to a *stronghold* (Psalm 27:1) or a *sure foundation* (Isaiah 33:6). The picture is clear: Danger exists all around us, our enemies surround us, but God is our safe place and refuge. In Him, danger is held at bay. We are safe.

The New Testament's use of *salvation* follows the same general pattern. It often has the sense of "establish" or "make firm." For example, Jesus tells His disciples, "All men will hate you because of Me, but he who stands firm to the end will be saved" (Matthew 10:22). Followers of Christ live in danger and opposition and salvation is standing firmly and securely in Christ. If we listen carefully, we hear echoes of God the fortress or rock. Perhaps a hint of the Old Testament's vivid metaphor also can be found in Jesus' exchange with the rich young man in Mark 10:17–31. To show the young, arrogant man how difficult it would be for a rich man to save himself, Jesus says, "It is easier for a camel to go through the eye of a needle than for a rich man to enter the kingdom of God" (Mark 10:25). Mark's account tells us that Jesus' disciples were amazed at this statement. They asked Jesus who could be saved. Jesus replied, "With man this is impossible, but not with God; all things are possible with God" (Mark 10:27). We simply have no way to save ourselves.

> Shadrach, Meshach and Abednego replied to the king, "O Nebuchadnezzar, we do not need to defend ourselves before you in this matter. If we are thrown into the blazing furnace, the God we serve is able to save us from it, and He will rescue us from your hand, O king. But even if He does not, we want you to know, O king, that we will not serve your gods or worship the image of gold you have set up." (Daniel 3:16–18)

I Walk in Danger All the Way

The world is a dangerous place. Our century has seen more deaths from war than all previous centuries combined. Many people experience danger from the threat of exposure to the elements. Countless numbers suffer and die as the victims of malnutrition and disease. The world of the 21st century, as always, is a dangerous world.

Even in our technologically advanced age, life is precarious. We no longer face daily danger from wild animals, and we are not nearly so vexed by the predations of illness, famine, flood, and sword, but new dangers abound. In the United States, even serene national parks can be places filled with danger and fear. It seems there is no safe place, no haven from the violence that surrounds us.

Though he lived in the 17th century, the composer who penned the hymn "I Walk in Danger All the Way" aptly described the life of a person living today. Officer Billings' precinct sergeant also was right: It is a war out there. What millions today don't know, however, is that the world is a much more dangerous place than it appears. The violence and chaos of our world have their roots in a much more profound and disturbing warfare that is taking place between God and His creatures. We are not simply at war with ourselves, we are at war with God. We are in danger not only from our fellow human beings, but we are in danger of God's righteous judgment. There is no safe place for sinners. "If You, O Lord, kept a record of sins, O Lord, who could stand?" (Psalm 130:3). We have no secure foundation on which to stand as we place ourselves in opposition to God. "But who can endure the day of His coming? Who can stand when He appears?" (Malachi 3:2).

The Power of God for Salvation

Thank God that Jesus has stood in our place and has turned away the wrath of God. God sent His only Son into the world not "to condemn the world, but to save the world through Him" (John 3:17). Jesus placed Himself in harm's way. He went to the most dangerous place in the world—to the cross of death—for the sins of the world so He could restore us to the safe haven of God's fortress. He endured the hatred of the world, the chaos of sin, and a violent death to save us from such a fate. He stood there for us so we might stand secure.

How wonderful! The "mighty arm of God" was nailed, weak and dying, to a cross. The "rock and fortress" poured out His blood in suffering and death. The fearless one underwent great agony in His passion so we might be strong, so we might be founded on the rock and stand courageous as we face the trials of life. How wonderful, but how ironic. Through weakness we are strengthened, through death we are brought to life. In answer to Paul's prayer to be relieved of his "thorn in the flesh," Jesus said, "My grace is sufficient for you, for My power is made perfect in weakness." Paul's response? "Therefore I will boast all the more gladly about my weaknesses, so that Christ's power may rest on me" (2 Corinthians 12:9).

> For the message of the cross is foolishness to those who are perishing, but to us who are being saved it is the power of God. (1 Corinthians 1:18)

This message of the Gospel—that Christ was put to death for our sins—is, as Paul writes, "the power of God for the salvation of everyone who believes" (Romans 1:16). It is powerful enough to overcome the greatest opposition, strong enough to calm the greatest fear. It is the "power of God," the "right hand and holy arm" of the one who came to be the Savior of the world. St. Peter makes a connection between God's salvation of Noah and his family from the danger and chaos of the flood (Genesis 6) and Baptism: "This water [that is, the flood] symbolizes baptism that now saves you" (1 Peter 3:21). Through the waters of Baptism, God saves us from chaos, danger, and death. He snatches us from the precipice, brings us back from the brink of disaster, calls us by name, delivers us from certain destruction, and carries us into the loving and safe arms of our Deliverer. We still may encounter danger in our lives, and we may face many fears, but through our Baptism, we are enabled to declare with Isaiah: "See, your Savior comes!" (Isaiah 62:11).

ENDNOTE

1. The Old Testament word translated as "salvation" is *yasha*. The Greek word translated as "salvation" is *sōtēria*.

24

Liberation

The Spirit of the Sovereign LORD is on Me, because
the LORD has anointed Me to preach good news to the
poor. He has sent Me to bind up the brokenhearted,
to proclaim freedom for the captives and release from
darkness for the prisoners, to proclaim the year of the
LORD's favor and the day of vengeance of our God, to
comfort all who mourn. (Isaiah 61:1–2)

IMPRISONED

Billy Lawrence learned the hard way what a precious
thing freedom was. He learned by losing his freedom. From
his jail cell, he could look out on the world. He saw the prison
guards and other workers coming and going freely while he
was imprisoned—for four years.

On the outside, Billy had taken freedom for granted. He
had been too free with his time, getting mixed up with the
wrong crowd. He started with petty theft, then graduated to
grand theft auto. Now his time was not his own. It would be
two more years before he was eligible for parole. He would be
30 years old before he got out. What a waste!

Billy missed his family, especially his mother. He would
give anything to be with her now in their home by the beach.

When he thought about it, he could almost feel the sun and the warm ocean breezes on his face. Instead, all he saw was the cold, dark, colorless cement walls of his cell. He yearned for liberation.

One day as Billy was attending a Bible study on his cell block, the chaplain read from Isaiah 61:1: "He has sent Me to bind up the brokenhearted, to proclaim freedom for the captives and release from darkness for the prisoners." The phrases "freedom for the captives" and "release for the prisoners" echoed in Billy's mind. How could this be?

The chaplain helped Billy to understand that, even though he remained a prisoner in jail, he could be freed from the spiritual prison of sin through faith in Jesus Christ. The chaplain told Billy that this was a freedom far greater than any earthly freedom he could know. It could help Billy deal with his current imprisonment. It also could help Billy to live a life of freedom when he was released from prison. Billy never had thought of it that way before. He decided to ask the chaplain to help him look into the Bible's promise of genuine freedom a bit more.

THE LORD SETS PRISONERS FREE

Another aspect of the deliverance metaphors is that God *liberates* us from imprisonment.[1] Similar to the *ransom* metaphor (in which God pays the price to release slaves from their captivity to an evil and oppressive taskmaster), *liberation* involves not the payment of a price for freedom, but the freeing of a prisoner by means of a powerful act.[2]

In Scripture, the image of freeing prisoners often refers to those in prison through no direct fault of their own. They are in prison as servants of God, oppressed by God's enemies. God's servant is bound in chains, wasting away in prison, unable to free himself. In this sense, the *liberation* metaphor does not directly address those in prison because of their own infraction of the law. Christ will not free all prisoners generally, though as we will see, there is relevance to those who languish in "prisons" of their own making.

In Scripture, lack of freedom is not the philosophically-oriented understanding of the Stoics, who basically maintained that lack of freedom was lack of control over life. Rather, existence itself is deficient and in a way "imprisoned." Paul writes: "For the creation was subjected to frustration, not by its own choice, but by the will of the one who subjected it, in hope that the creation itself will be liberated from its bondage to decay and brought into the glorious freedom of the children of God" (Romans 8:20–21). Humans are in prison because they live in a world—creation itself—that lies in "frustration" and "bondage to decay." From this, God frees us in Christ the Deliverer.

> In my anguish I cried to the LORD, and He answered by setting me free. The LORD is with me; I will not be afraid. What can man do to me? The LORD is with me; He is my helper. (Psalm 118:5–7a)

BONDAGE TO DECAY

This way of saying the Gospel may well be unintelligible to many people in western society. We have so many freedoms that we never would admit to being less than fully free. In America, freedom is the greatest good, protected by the Constitution. Freedom of religion, freedom of speech, freedom of the press, freedom of assembly—these are cherished foundations of our "free society." "Live Free or Die" is the motto of New Hampshire. "Give me liberty or give me death" is the striking ultimatum of the American Revolution. To sell Americans on the idea that they are "subjected to frustration" and in "bondage to decay" is a hard sell indeed. We are free, we assume, and subject to no one.

On the other hand, there are more people in prison in the United States today than ever before. More than 1.5 million men are incarcerated in state and federal prison systems.

Untold numbers—including family and friends of inmates—know firsthand what it is like to lose freedom and languish in prison. Furthermore, all people know what it's like to be in a situation beyond their control, stuck in a dead-end job, lost in a fruitless relationship, or suffering under financial constraints of various kinds. We all can relate to the feeling of being imprisoned.

What people don't know, however, and what Billy came to understand, is that we are in prison because of our own doing. We live in the prison of a fallen world, given over to sin and death. What is worse, we don't even realize it. Believing we are free, we are subject to futility, just like the creation over which we imagine we are "lords." Imagine the sad irony: We think we are free when we gain sovereignty over a creation that is itself in prison and without freedom. We are rulers, free to roam in a concentration camp. Our vaunted freedom is only a delusion, and it only makes our imprisonment worse. We are in "bondage to decay." There is nothing worse—and nothing more dangerous—than a convict who thinks he's free.

THE GLORIOUS FREEDOM

When we recognize our spiritual imprisonment, we can begin to glimpse the "glorious freedom" (Romans 8:21) God has in store for us through Christ Jesus. The freedom given through faith in Christ is not the kind of static, philosophical freedom of the political scientists (as important as it may be for a fruitful and satisfying life in society). There is a definite directionality about the freedom of Christ.

First, Christ provides us with a freedom *from*. He frees us from the oppression of sin, death, and the power of the devil. St. Paul writes: "Through Christ Jesus the law of the Spirit of life set me free from the law of sin and death" (Romans 8:2). Christ has provided a great liberation from the forces that held us fast in their grasp. He brought us genuine freedom.

Christ also has freed us from the need to merit salvation before God. "It is for freedom that Christ has set us free," Paul declares (Galatians 5:1). We have been liberated from the obligation to justify ourselves. Christ already has done that for us. Christ has done it *all* for us. He has entered into the prison of our fallen world. He was subjected to the sentence for our sin, and He suffered capital punishment in our place. He "went to the chair" for us. We are, therefore, free from the need to undergo the punishment we deserved, free from "serving time."

> Therefore, there is now no condemnation for those who are in Christ Jesus, because through Christ Jesus the law of the Spirit of life set me free from the law of sin and death. (Romans 8:1–2)

Second, we are free *for* a life of discipleship. Jesus Himself says, "If the Son sets you free, you will be free indeed" (John 8:36). Genuine freedom is not the kind of absolute freedom to live life as one wants to, a common aspiration among Americans. Rather, true freedom is to live life as God wills, as God intended us originally to live. St. Peter writes: "Live as free men, but do not use your freedom as a cover-up for evil; live as servants of God" (1 Peter 2:16). Christians don't need their good works; they have the perfect good works of Jesus as their own through faith. We are free to give our good works away to others, who do need them, sometimes desperately.

Jesus has provided a great liberation to those who through faith live in Him. He has not, however, freed us from the damaging consequences of our sinful actions. When Christians commit crimes, as Billy did, they go to jail. When they make poor business decisions, they suffer the consequences. At other times Christians suffer curtailment of their liberty for reasons that are not their fault. Either way, through faith in Christ, believers are "brought into the glorious freedom of the children of God" (Romans 8:21).

Endnotes

1. The Greek word translated as "freedom" is *eulutheria*.
2. A considerable amount of overlap exists between the commerce and deliverance metaphors. Although the commerce context seems to be more common, deliverance overtones are frequent throughout the Bible.

25

Victory

This is the victory that has overcome the world, even our faith. Who is it that overcomes the world? Only he who believes that Jesus is the Son of God. (1 John 5:4–5)

DEFEATED

"I just can't believe that!" Antoine Jordan told his mother. "No way I can go for a God like that." For Antoine, the Jesus he learned about in Sunday school was too weak, too humble. He never would survive a single day on the South Side.

If Antoine had learned anything in his 15 years of life in the city, it was that you had to be strong. Show no fear. Don't give an inch. Never display any sign of weakness. If you did, it meant certain defeat. The gangs would eat you for lunch. A God who was weak and merciful might play in the burbs, but not in his neighborhood. That's why Antoine stopped going to church, even though his mother was always after him to attend. He didn't know how Jesus could help him on the streets. Besides, guys made fun of guys who went to church. Church was for women and girls, not for men.

One day, however, Antoine heard that Robert Williams, his favorite basketball player, was coming to town. He would be talking at a local church. Antoine had long idolized Williams. He had all the moves: He could dribble and pass and shoot like no one else. He was a winner, a real success, a symbol of power. He even had his own line of basketball shoes.

What Antoine heard when he attended Williams' speech, however, shocked him. Williams quoted a Bible passage: "Everyone born of God overcomes the world" (1 John 5:4). Williams said that without Jesus, he considered himself a loser. He gave Jesus credit for all his success on and off the court. He said that you didn't need to join gangs. True victory comes through faith in Christ.

What's this about a victory that overcomes the world? Antoine thought. *How could that be true? I thought faith was for little girls and old women. I thought you had to be weak to be a member of a church. I thought Jesus was just this mild, middle-class, white guy. Is it possible to be a winner and a Christian at the same time?*

THE VICTORY THAT OVERCOMES THE WORLD

A final aspect of the deliverance metaphors is *victory.*[1] This is an uncommon way to say the Gospel, but it is striking in certain contexts. The background of this word is a contest in which God provides the victory. It may be spoken of as a war or a struggle against the forces of chaos. This metaphor also is applied to the spiritual battle going on between God and the "principalities and powers" of this world.[2] At other times, the enemy against which Jesus wages war is death, as when Paul exults: "Where, O death, is your victory?" (1 Corinthians 15:55).

Scripture is clear: A battle rages between Jesus and the world (1 John 5:4).[3] Jesus Himself says: "I have told you these things, so that in Me you may have peace. In this world you will have trouble. But take heart! I have overcome the world" (John 16:33). A particularly potent way to say the Gospel, therefore, is to say that Christ has engaged in battle with the forces of evil and has vanquished them, giving those who live in Him the victory.

Although this imagery is powerful and evocative, there are several ways to make this imagery too literal. In the Old Testament, part of God's salvation was to give His people victory over His and their enemies (Psalm 18:50). But the real antagonist in God's war, whether in ancient times or today, is a spiritual one. God wages war against any force, power, or being that would supplant Him as God and against anything that would attempt to separate us from God's love (Romans 8:39). It would, therefore, be pushing this metaphor too far to suggest that God physically wars against our enemies and literally vanquishes them.

In addition, it is hazardous to make a direct identification between our enemies (those who, for any reason, oppose us) and God's enemies. In Scripture, the enemies that the psalmists complain about are always also God's enemies; they oppose God's reign. On the other hand, because we are sinful, we make plenty of our own enemies, demonizing them to suit our own purposes.

It's wrong to understand God as a warlike God who relishes a good fight. Although God is ready to go to battle for those who are His own, we might say that He does so hesitantly. Thus, it is unseemly to depict God on the basis of this metaphor as a bloodthirsty warrior.[4] On the other hand, it would be equally wrong to depict Him as a weakling and a doormat. This metaphor tells us that God is a strong victor who will go to any length necessary to rescue His loved ones from the chaos and discord of death and the forces of this world. And He succeeds!

> I was pushed back and about to fall, but the Lord helped me. The Lord is my strength and my song; He has become my salvation. Shouts of joy and victory resound in the tents of the righteous: "The Lord's right hand has done mighty things! The Lord's right hand is lifted high; the Lord's right hand has done mighty things!" (Psalm 118:13–16)

Bruised Reeds and Smoldering Wicks

God is no pushover. But what about us? We don't like to admit defeat. No one wants to admit that they are weak and in need of help. We want to know the thrill of victory but not the agony of defeat. In many ways, the worst thing that could happen to us is that we are known as losers. We all want to be on the winning team. Our society is so saturated with notions of winning and success that we hardly notice the damaging effects these ideas have on us. We simply take it for granted. The losing coach gets fired. The losing player gets traded. For people like Antoine, winning is more than a luxury. Winning gets you more than bragging rights. Winning means survival. In Antoine's context, losers die. Weakness and defeat are harmful to your health.

For these reasons, the malady behind the *victory* metaphor is a difficult one for people to admit. We do not want to admit that we are weak or losers. But before God, that's exactly what we are. All of us are victims of powers and forces beyond our control. We all have our weaknesses, our oppressors, that we are unable to overcome: addictions, poverty, crime, dead-end jobs. We are imprisoned by harmful lifestyles. Try as we will, we cannot raise ourselves out of our situation. The forces against us are too strong. We can't contend with the world's captivation and the enthralling "powers and authorities."

Isaiah 42:3–4 speaks of us as "a bruised reed" and a "smoldering wick." The imagery is vivid. We are weak blades of grass, blown in the wind before the powers of this world. We are candles flickering with subdued light, almost at the point of extinction before the powers that be. We are in their grasp, and we cannot free ourselves. The more we struggle, the deeper we fall into the snares of the devil and the more defeated we become. It will take someone stronger than ourselves to give us the victory from our spiritual imprisonment.

Hyper-Conquerors!

The strong one is our Lord Jesus Christ. He rushes to our defense and conquers our enemies—sin, death, and the power of the devil. With Paul, we can thrill in the good news: "But thanks be to God! He gives us the victory through our Lord Jesus Christ" (1 Corinthians 15:57). The victory is ours through Christ the Victor!

There is nothing weak or insipid about Christ's victory. It is real; it is present. But the victory also now directs our attention forward to the future, to the day of the resurrection. The victory is ours *now* through faith, but we may not necessarily see the victory by sight. We still experience weakness, defeat, and even death, as all people certainly will, unless the Lord comes first. Our victory in Christ today by faith is in an anticipation of that great day when "death has been swallowed up in victory" (1 Corinthians 15:54).

One of America's most well-known icons is the Nike Swoosh logo, which adorns athletic equipment and clothes worn by some of the world's best and most successful athletes. *Nike* is the English spelling of the Greek word for "victory." In an interesting twist, St. Paul uses the Greek word *nike* in Romans 8 as a way of emphasizing the decisiveness and certainty of Christ's victory over the powers and dominions. Paul writes: "Who shall separate us from the love of Christ? Shall trouble or hardship or persecution or famine or nakedness or danger or sword? ... No, in all these things we are more than conquerors through Him who loved us" (Romans 8:35, 37). In Greek, "more than conquerors" is a contraction of two words: *hyper* and *conquerors.* Paul goes Nike one better. We are not merely conquerors, we are hyper-conquerors through Christ. Our standing is firm, our future secure, through Him who loved us, our Hyper-Victor, Jesus Christ.

ENDNOTES

1. The Greek word translated as "victory" is *nike.*

2. Paul refers to these "powers" in various ways. For example, in Romans 8:38, he calls them simply "powers." In Ephesians 1:21, he calls them "all ... power and dominion." In Colossians 2:10, he calls them "every power and authority." In Ephesians 2:2, he refers to "the ruler of the kingdom of the air, the spirit who is now at work in those who are disobedient."

3. When Jesus is said to be in opposition to the world, or the "powers" of this world, care must be taken not to confuse the biblical, Christian teaching with a form of pagan dualism, which would suggest that there are two equally matched powers—good and evil—which are in constant battle with each other over the souls of humans. While the powers of the evil one, Satan, are real and considerable, Satan is no match for Christ. Thus, Jesus said, "I have overcome the world" (John 16:33). Nor should we think of the world as being irredeemably evil or turned over to satanic powers. The world, though fallen and corrupted by sin, is still "God's world," which He loved enough to send His Son to save (John 3:16–17).

4. A great deal of mischief and harm has been done throughout the history of the church by depicting God as a warrior, from the crusades and holy wars of the Middle Ages to the religious conflicts of today.

PART 8

THE WORLD MISSION
AND THE GOSPEL'S WORDS

26

God's Mission in Words

> We do, however, speak a message of wisdom among
> the mature, but not the wisdom of this age or of the
> rulers of this age, who are coming to nothing. No, we
> speak of God's secret wisdom, a wisdom that has been
> hidden and that God destined for our glory before time
> began. (1 Corinthians 2:6–7)

The biblical metaphors for the Gospel are rich. God has
given us a tremendous depth of language through His inspired
writers to know the wonders of what He has done for us in His
Son, Jesus Christ.

After examining the metaphors themselves, we explore
the fact that the Gospel's universality is demonstrated in its
words. We examine the nature of words, especially the Words
of God, as a way of reaching beyond ourselves.

THE UNIVERSALITY OF THE GOSPEL
AND THE UNIVERSALITY OF ITS WORDS

There are many ways to say the Gospel. In its diversity,
the Gospel overcomes cultural and linguistic barriers. There
is a universality about the Gospel not only in the sense that
God "wants all men to be saved and to come to a knowledge
of the truth" (1 Timothy 2:4), but also in the fact that the very

language of the Gospel is universal. The Gospel's universality, therefore, is found not only in its substance, but also in its form; not only in its broad content, but also in its specific words. Francis Rossow writes:

> God uses gospel-metaphors ... to reach all kinds of people. What may not be effective on a particular person might be effective on another. Whereas a certain culture may be impervious to one approach, it may be open to another.[1]

For this reason, it may be helpful to explore a bit deeper the relationship between the language of the Gospel and the universality or catholicity of the church as it relates to the mission of God. The word *catholic* means "universal," in the sense of "according to the totality" or "in keeping with the whole."[2] The church is catholic in a double sense. First, it is catholic because Christ is present in her through His Gospel in its various forms—verbal (spoken, written, proclaimed) and sacramental (Baptism and the Lord's Supper). Where Christ Jesus and the Word about Him are, there is the catholic church. In the church, the fullness of Christ's body is found, united with its head, which implies that the church receives from Christ the fullness of salvation in the Word and sacraments. The church was, in this fundamental sense, catholic, or universal, on the day of Pentecost. Although divided by external disunity, the church remains catholic until the day our Lord returns. The church is universal because Christ, the Church's Head, and His Gospel are universal.

Second, the church is catholic because she has been sent out by Christ on a mission to the entire human race. The mission is to proclaim that universal Gospel throughout all the world. There is, therefore, a universality about the church because the Gospel of Christ has this outward thrust. Universality characterizes the church, which ceaselessly seeks the ingathering of all people under Christ, her head, and in the unity of His Spirit.

Thus, the church has about it a twofold thrust, or impulse, that originates in the Gospel itself. By the Gospel, the church both calls inward to unity and it sends out to diversity. It is the Gospel that gathers and sends, that draws in and disperses.

By Word and sacraments, particularly by Baptism, Christ draws His own to Himself and incorporates them into Himself. Likewise, motivated by the Gospel, Christ sends His own out into the world to live out their vocations in His Name.[3] The church is guided by the Gospel in her internal relations (for example, inter-Christian relationships), as well as her external relations (for example, evangelism, missions, and inter-religious dialogue). Each of these "impulses"—ingathering and out-sending—is a necessary component of the universality of the church.

The universality of the church is brought about by the universality of the Gospel by which the church lives and on which she depends for her very existence. Yet the language of the Gospel is an ignored dimension of the catholicity of the church or of the universality of the Gospel. The substance of the faith, the article on which the church stands and falls, has many ways of being said, ways that transcend linguistic, social, and cultural barriers. The language is *catholic*. The metaphors are *universal*. They cut across what divides us as human beings. There is not a people-group in the world to which the Gospel is utterly incomprehensible. We have a way of saying it that will make sense, that will be intelligible, to every person. If one way of saying it doesn't make sense, another way will.

Thus the Gospel is universal not only in its substance, but also in its form (its language). The church is catholic because the Gospel is catholic. The Gospel is catholic because, in part, its language is catholic. The complexity of communicating the essence of Christianity or of the Gospel to the world's diverse cultures is staggering. But we take a great step forward when we more completely use the universality imbedded in the language of the Gospel itself.

Christ commanded that His disciples go into all the world so "repentance and forgiveness of sins will be preached in His

211

name to all nations" (Luke 24:47). Yet the Gospel does not merely "go out," as if into thin air. It goes out into specific contexts, into beautifully diverse social, cultural, linguistic, and racial settings. An important part of the universality of the Gospel is that it makes its home in so many diverse places. It does so through its beautiful words.

For it to be the Gospel of God, the Gospel must be enfleshed in human words. As Christ has two natures—divine and human—so His Word, the Gospel, has two natures, also divine and human. For Jesus to be the Christ of Scriptures who has saved and justified us, the human nature is necessary. It is not merely an afterthought; His human nature is of the very essence of the Christ, the incarnate God. Likewise, the human nature of the Gospel is necessary for it to be the Gospel of God. It must be incarnated in human language. If it is to be the propitiating Gospel, it must be enfleshed in human words and categories and metaphors.

The human dimension of the Gospel, therefore, is not a necessary evil. It is the very essence of the Gospel and necessary for it to be truly the Gospel. This implies everything for our proclamation of the Gospel. It means that we must give close attention to the words, their formulation, their metaphorical value, their evocative powers. To slight the human nature of the Gospel by diminishing the importance and necessity of words in our proclamation is to commit an egregious error that in the end may render it no longer the Gospel that reconciles sinners. The universality of the Gospel results not only from the divine power with which it is endowed by the Spirit of God, but also in no small measure from its character as human language.

WORDS AS A WAY
OF REACHING BEYOND OURSELVES

The very act of speaking or communicating verbally can be understood as a way to transcend ourselves. Speaking is an

essentially social task. It requires an "other." Speaking to ourselves is not a dialogue; it is a monologue. It is not truly speaking in the sense of connecting verbally with another. Thus,
God has supplied us with a form of the Gospel—that is, with
words—that is fundamentally other-oriented.

The major part of the "transcendental" character of the
Gospel is that it is a Word, empowered by the Holy Spirit, that
gives us entree to God. The Gospel Word tells us how things
are between us and God, and thus we are given a way to reach
beyond, to transcend our humanness. In short, we receive a
divine perspective from the divine Word.

But the Gospel spoken or written through metaphors
also enables us to reach beyond ourselves. Metaphors provide
access into the real world as it is. What is true of metaphors is
generally true of all language. We apprehend reality and transcend our individuality, in part, through words. The world of
the outside is brought inside our minds through words, which
are evocative of an entire world outside ourselves.

In a very real sense, we have access to the world through
words. If this is true of words in general, it is certainly true of
the words that are the Word of God. We come to the Word of
God, or it comes to us, through human words and not apart
from them. So the words themselves must be taken with the
utmost seriousness if we hope to convey the divine, saving
Word to others. That's the way the Word of God works. It
comes in words. It cannot be communicated to others without
them.

The world's many languages have many distinctive words
that are peculiar to each dialect and not intelligible to those
unfamiliar with the language. So it is not in the external signs,
the vocables, where what transcends individuality is found,
but in what is conveyed by the signifier. That is what is so powerful about metaphors. While the vocable that references them
is different in every language (life, *vida*, *Leben*, *vie*), what is
conveyed is universal. Every language knows what *life* is, and

by whatever term in whatever language, the same thing is evoked.

Metaphors evoke things that are universal, transcendental, and necessary. The creation metaphors bring to mind things pertaining to life, existence, health, nourishment, growth. The commerce metaphors elicit thoughts of value and worth. The legal metaphors evoke every person's need for order, for setting things right, for control. The personal metaphors highlight every person's need for unity and belonging. The sacrificial metaphors raise to the foreground the need all people have for a sense of dignity and sanctity. The deliverance metaphors point out the basic need of every person to be safe from violence or chaos.

Every metaphor touches on something primal, something universal. In its own way, each one speaks to a transcendental need. Each provides us with a way to reach beyond ourselves and to connect with something greater, something larger than our particularity. This simple dimension of the Gospel provides an effective foundation for the communication of the Good News, whether to those in or outside the church.

Preaching or Speaking the Gospel's Words

Pastors are called by God and their congregations to preach a new sermon every week (and sometimes more than once a week!). They often have a great deal of difficulty preparing new, fresh material each time. This is made more difficult when pastors follow a lectionary and preach on the same appointed texts every few years. Preachers complain of burnout. As they often say, "The well has run dry."

Pastors may run into two opposing but equally dangerous temptations. To remain faithful to the Gospel, they resort to saying the Gospel the same way each time, over and over again, week in and week out. Alternatively, to retain freshness in preaching, they seek new idioms or categories other than the traditional ones. In the first case, pastors put their hearers at risk of losing interest in the Gospel. In the second instance, pastors put their hearers at risk of not hearing the Gospel at all because innovation has surrendered the substance of the Gospel. Neither option is acceptable. Both have harmful effects on hearers.

Appreciating the metaphorical value of the Gospel's words can go a long way toward reducing these two temptations. Although preparing a solid, Law and Gospel sermon is hard work and requires a great deal of time, it can be made easier if the words themselves are kept in mind and the Gospel is preached with the metaphorical color and richness implicit in these words. The Bible is a veritable treasure chest of rich and diverse language with which to proclaim the Gospel. It is not necessary to preach the Gospel the same way every time or to come up with a new way of saying it every time. Creative preaching of the Gospel as metaphor will be both faithful to the texts and interesting to hearers.

Preaching the Gospel as metaphor is textual. It is based on sound principles of historical and grammatical interpretation of Holy Scripture. It finds the meaning of a text in the words. It does not impose words or meaning on the text, but rather draws the meaning out of the passage itself. Every unit and every passage of Scripture contain one or more of these metaphors. The preacher's task is simply to explicate the text by choosing one of the metaphors, the dominant metaphor (if there is one), and crafting the sermon around it. Although the preacher may make a number of applications or associations arising from the metaphor, it is still a biblical, textual sermon because the beginning point is always the words of the text.

Preaching the Gospel as metaphor is also interesting. There is a sharpness or vividness to understanding the Gospel as metaphor that is not there if the words are understood in a flat, generic theology way. These living metaphors free our words from their captivity to generalization and spiritualizing; the Gospel no longer is viewed as "church-talk" or "preacher's language." Such preaching gives the words free course to find a home in the minds and imaginations of hearers, which will result in joy and edification. At the same time, it enables the preacher to remain faithful to the texts of the Bible. Finally, it makes preaching enjoyable as the expositor of Holy Writ explores the depths of Scripture and mines its verbal treasures. Not incidentally, it makes the hearing of the Gospel enjoyable, too, as hearers are taken up into the world of the Gospel's words proclaimed creatively by their faithful pastor.

ECUMENICAL DIALOGUE

The Scriptures speak the Gospel in many ways. Throughout the history of the church, the Gospel also has been said in many ways by the various Christian traditions. Each tradition has had its favorite metaphors and images. Lutherans and the classical Reformed[4] have tended to focus on the legal metaphors as primary ways to say the Gospel. They have emphasized the forensic and objective aspects of the Gospel that were lacking in the medieval concepts of salvation.

Roman Catholics have tended to focus on the sacrificial and creation metaphors. Their emphasis on the distance of God, necessitating a priestly intermediary, and their understanding of the Mass as an "unbloody sacrifice" on the altar stem from the central place they give to the sacrificial metaphors. The importance they place on the necessity of good works and the overlap between justification and sanctification attests to the vital role the creation metaphors play in Roman Catholic thinking.[5] The commerce metaphors also have played an important role in Catholic theology, as evident in the emphasis on the purchasing of masses for the release of the faithful dead from time in purgatory.[6]

Methodists and Holiness groups, with their emphasis on the importance of leading a holy life, tend to rely on the sacrificial language of sanctifying and hallowing. They frequently use the language of cleansing to emphasize the *result* of Christ's work in the believer and to stress that God requires a morally upright and perfect life.

Baptists and many Pentecostal groups, for whom conversion is the defining moment of faith, draw on the *birth* metaphor. They stress the necessity of being "born again," which signifies an abrupt break with the sinful past and a radical turnaround in lifestyle. This is symbolized by a baptism in which they "make a decision for Christ" or "accept Him" or "give themselves" to Him.

Eastern Orthodox Christians, like Roman Catholics, focus more on the transformational metaphors—language that describes the life-changes the Gospel works in people. In addition, they give a prominent place to the legal metaphors, especially *justification.* However, they make different use of this metaphor than Lutherans and Reformed Christians. For the Orthodox, the primary emphasis is on God's cosmic establishment of order out of chaos. For Orthodox Christians, order and hierarchy in a chaotic world are a principal good. For classical Reformation theology, the emphasis is on the courtroom declaration of the judge.

Each denomination or theological tradition has had its dominant metaphor by which it understands and makes sense of God's saving work in Christ. Where one metaphor has been allowed to dominate to the exclusion of the others, however, distortion and error have arisen. The obvious answer is not to allow one metaphor to dominate the others, thus reducing each metaphor's contribution to the whole, but to use them all. Each metaphor has something irreplaceable to contribute to the fullness of the Gospel. Each is necessary.

Because each major Christian tradition has had its primary way to speak the Gospel, the church today is enriched as we dialogue with one another in our respective denominations. No one tradition can claim exclusive right to the Gospel's fullness. We may learn more about ourselves by examining more critically how we tend to say and hear the Gospel in light of how others say it.

To clarify the ways we speak the Gospel by honoring its language will not necessarily resolve the ecumenical impasse. There remain intractable difficulties between the various traditions within Christianity. For example, in addition to divergent understandings of the Gospel, there also are divergent understandings of other key doctrines, such as church and sacraments, though these differences may not be so apparent. In fact, it is possible that many of these other theological differences between the denominations have their root in differences about speaking the Gospel.

Nevertheless, it would help immensely if we were to use our various ways to say the Gospel as a means of pointing toward a way out of the ecumenical impasse. At the very least, it would focus our attention on the center of all Christian theology: how to say what our loving Father has done for us in Christ, His Son. Clarity of language is not the whole solution, but it is an essential first step.

EVANGELISM

Taking the Gospel's words seriously and giving them their full value has great potential for the church's evangelistic task. In the chapter scenarios, it became apparent that a given metaphor is particularly suited to a given situation. The best way to say the Gospel to someone depends on the situation—a person's experiences, age, emotional state, or stage of life.

The *life* metaphor, of course, is particularly meaningful at the beginning or end of life. It also is highly meaningful to a person struggling with ecological or environmental issues. The *birth* metaphor might be heard with particular force by a person in a nursing home. Through the Gospel, we bring light to those in the darkness of evil or ignorance, bread and water to those who lack, salvation to those who are unhealthy or who live or work in dangerous places. Through God's Good News, we hold out redemption to the poor, justification for the guilty, reconciliation for those enduring divisions, cleansing to those who are dirty, victory to the defeated.

The possibilities are endless. What we need for the effective and relevant announcement of the Gospel, particularly in evangelism, is to glance at the situation of our audience. The first tasks are to look and listen. How are people experiencing life's burdens? How do they experience the Law? Do they experience it as hunger, thirst, inner despair, not belonging, unholiness, ignorance? We begin where they are. Effective evangelism begins with silence. It happens well when people care enough to hear the cry of others, to hear how others understand reality, and to speak the comforting words of the Gospel to that reality.

To speak the Gospel effectively to neighbors, coworkers, or fellow students does not require a prepackaged program of evangelism. We need familiarity with the richness and breadth of the biblical language of the Gospel and a sensitive ear. The Scriptures present us with words that speak to our realities in unique, often very personal, ways. Opportunities to speak Good News cannot always be predicted. Evangelism is not usually packaged. Outreach happens as we share the Gospel (with its "human nature") and connect it with people as they are able to hear it.

MISSIONS

Missions is the "last frontier" of the Gospel. Mission is essential to the church's life and ministry. Ultimately, of course, the Lord's missionary mandate is grounded in the eternal love of the Holy Trinity. The church is, by her nature, missionary because, according to the will of the Father, she has her origin in the *missio*—the sending—of the Son and the Holy Spirit. The ultimate purpose of mission is none other than to make all sinners share in the communion between the Father and the Son and the Holy Spirit. This occurs through the sending out—the mission—of the Gospel in the Word and sacraments, particularly Baptism. As Christ said in Matthew 28, Baptism is, together with His Word, the means of gathering all those scattered and led astray by sin into this blessed communion with the Triune God. Mission is a necessary implication of the church's universality.

The Gospel is at the center of God's mission in the world. This Gospel is universal. It is universal because it is intended for all. God wants all to be saved and to come to the knowledge of the truth in Christ. It is universal because Christ's atonement avails for all—for the entire world. But the Gospel also is universal in the sense that it is communicated through universal categories, through metaphors and language that are universally understandable.

Victor Raj has written: "There is no single successful method for relating the Gospel of Jesus Christ to any particular people or culture."[7] This is undoubtedly true. To reach any culture or people-group, it will be necessary to say the Gospel in many ways, ways that may, according to time or place, strike the ears of sinners as relevant. Among other ways, this is seen in the fact that each Christian tradition has its favorite way to say the Gospel. Each metaphor strikes a chord or appeals in a unique way, according to how each tradition feels the Gospel needs to be heard in a particular time or place.

It probably also is true, however, that there is no single successful method for relating the Gospel to all peoples or cultures. Not all cultures will respond readily to, for example, the forensic, or legal, metaphors. Not all cultures are able to comprehend these metaphors. Some will understand more readily the creation metaphors or the personal metaphors. Some will more readily grasp the sacrificial metaphors. While it is true that no one way to say the Gospel will encompass all that can be or must be said concerning the Gospel, it is also true that one or another metaphor will provide an especially relevant or meaningful way to comprehend the Gospel in a specific culture. One metaphor may not be universally comprehensive, nor may it be universally comprehensible, but it may be comprehensible locally.

The primary impetus to the church's missionary endeavors is that the Father sent His Son into the world and the Son has sent the church into all the world. An additional impetus, however, is found in the words with which Christ sends us into the world. The words themselves, simply because they are words, have an outward impulse. Because they evoke transcendental significance, they prompt us to reach beyond ourselves. Words *must* go out, they *must* go forth. That is their nature.

Yet the words with which Christians go out into all the world are not just words. They can never be just words because they are the very words of Christ, the Word of the Gospel, "the power of God for the salvation of everyone who believes" (Romans 1:16). The words themselves are powerful, rich, and evocative, not just words. They are words that make us just.

ENDNOTES

1. Francis Rossow, *Preaching the Creative Gospel Creatively* (St. Louis: Concordia Publishing House, 1983), 34.

2. *The Catechism of the Catholic Church* (Mahwah, NJ: Paulist Press, 1994), 220–227.

3. *Vocation* is a rich and penetrating way to understand one's life in Christ. Even in the most trivial, everyday things, believers see themselves in a holy calling (vocation), appointed by God.

4. The word *Reformed* historically referred to the followers of Jean Calvin, the Swiss reformer and author of *The Institutes of the Christian Religion*. Although not many of them claim to be strict followers of Calvin, Reformed denominations in North America today would include various Presbyterian, United Church of Christ, Reformed Church of America, and Dutch Reformed congregations.

5. Roman Catholics tend to stress so-called "transformational" language—such as *life, enlightenment, nourishment,* etc.—which emphasizes the change brought about in the Christian.

6. This was a primary cause of the Reformation. Martin Luther posted his 95 Theses to protest the sale of indulgences that could "purchase" forgiveness.

7. Victor Raj, *The Hindu Connection: Roots of the New Age* (St. Louis: Concordia Publishing House, 1995), 123.

Appendix
Scripture References for Further Study

CHAPTER 3: BIRTH
John 1:12–13
  1:18
1 Corinthians 4:15
Philemon 10
Titus 3:3–7
James 1:15–18
1 Peter 1:3
  1:23–25
1 John 3:9
  4:7
  5:1

CHAPTER 4: LIFE
Leviticus 18:5
Deuteronomy 8:3
  32:47
Job 19:25
Psalm 16:9ff
  49:16ff
  73:23ff
Proverbs 9:6
Isaiah 26:19
  53:10–12
  55:3

Ezekiel 18:32
  37:1–14
Daniel 12:2–3
Amos 5:4, 14
John 1:1, 4
  5:21
  5:24
  6:63
  6:68
  8:12
  10:10
  11:25–26
  14:6
Romans 4:17
  5:15–21
  6:1–11
  8:10–11
1 Corinthians 15:20–23
  15:44–49
  15:53–57
Galatians 2:19–20
Ephesians 2:4–5
Colossians 2:13
1 John 3:14
  5:11–12

CHAPTER 5: SALVATION
Matthew 9:22
Mark 5:34
10:46–52
Luke 8:48
17:19
18:42
John 9:30–41
James 5:15

CHAPTER 6: LIGHT
Genesis 1:3
Numbers 6:25
Psalm 18:28
19:8
27:1
36:9
37:6
43:3
56:13
119:105
Isaiah 8:22–9:2
42:6
45:7
49:6
60:1–3
60:19–21
61:1
Matthew 4:16
6:22–23
17:1–9
Luke 2:29–32

John 1:6–8

3:19–21
5:35
8:12
9:5
12:35–36
12:46
2 Corinthians 4:4–6
Ephesians 5:8, 14
Colossians 1:12–13
1 Thessalonians 5:4–9
2 Timothy 1:10
1 Peter 2:9
1 John 1:5, 7
2:8–11
Revelation 21:23
22:5

CHAPTER 7: BREAD AND WATER
Bread
Deuteronomy 8:3
Matthew 4:4
5:6
6:11
John 6:33–51
1 Corinthians 11:23–28
Water
Psalm 1:3
23:2
Isaiah 12:3
32:2
49:10
55:1
58:11
Jeremiah 17:8

31:9
Zechariah 14:8
John 3:5
4:4–26
7:38
Ephesians 10:22
1 John 5:6
Revelation 7:17
21:6
22:17

CHAPTER 8: RANSOM
Exodus 6:6–8
13:13
15:13
30:12
Numbers 3:44–51
31:51
Psalm 49:7–9
Isaiah 35:9–10
50:2
51:10–11
Jeremiah 31:11
Hosea 13:14
Matthew 20:28
Mark 10:45
Luke 1:68–79
2:38
18:7
21:28
24:21
Romans 3:21–26
8:23
1 Corinthians 1:30

Ephesians 1:3–14
4:30
Colossians 1:13–14
1 Timothy 2:5–6
Titus 2:13–14
Hebrews 9:12
9:15
11:35
1 Peter 1:18–21

CHAPTER 9: REDEMPTION
Deuteronomy 7:7–9
9:26
13:5
15:15
21:8
24:18
Ruth 4
2 Samuel 7:23
1 Chronicles 17:21
Job 19:25
Psalm 19:14
34:22
49:7–9
49:15
74:2
77:15
103:4
106:10
111:9
130:7–8

Isaiah 1:27
43:1
44:6
44:21–23
48:17, 20
52: 3, 9
59:20
62:12
63:9
Hosea 13:14
Micah 4:10
Matthew 13:44–46
Romans 3:24
1 Corinthians 6:19–20
7:23
Galatians 3:13
4:4–5
2 Peter 2:1
Revelation 5:9
14:3–4

CHAPTER 10: PROPERTY
Exodus 19:5
Deuteronomy 7:6
14:2
Psalm 130:8
135:4
Malachi 3:17
Acts 20:28
Romans 3:24
1 Corinthians 6:20
Ephesians 1:3–14
2 Thessalonians 2:13–14
Titus 2:13–14
1 Peter 2:9

CHAPTER 11: FORGIVENESS/
REMISSION
Hosea 6:6
Matthew 5:7
6:12
9:13
18:23–35
Luke 7:36–50
James 2:13

CHAPTER 12: JUSTIFICATION
Genesis 5:16
Isaiah 46:13
53:11
Jeremiah 23:5–6
Matthew 5:6
6:33
Luke 1:75
Romans 1:17
3:21–25ff
4:3
4:5
4:22–25
5:1
5:9
5:16
5:18–19
6:18
8:10
8:30
8:33
9:30–32
10:3–4
1 Corinthians 6:11

2 Corinthians 5:21
Galatians 2:16
  2:21
  3:11
  5:5
Philippians 3:9
2 Timothy 4:8
Titus 3:5–7
1 Peter 2:24
  3:18
1 John 1:19

CHAPTER 13: INTERCESSION
Isaiah 53:12
  59:15–16
John 14:16
  14:25
  15:26
  16:7
Romans 8:26–27
  8:34
Galatians 3:19–20
1 Timothy 2:5
Hebrews 7:25
  9:24
1 John 2:1

CHAPTER 14: ADOPTION
Exodus 4:22
  6:7
Psalm 2:7
John 1:12–13
Romans 8:15–23
  9:4
Galatians 4:5ff

Ephesians 1:4–5

CHAPTER 15: INHERITANCE
Matthew 5:3
  21:33–46
  25:34
Mark 10:17
  12:1–12
Luke 20:9–19
Acts 20:32
Romans 4:13–15
  8:17
1 Corinthians 15:50
2 Corinthians 5:5
Galatians 3:18
  3:26–4:7
Ephesians 1:14
  1:18
  5:5
Colossians 1:12
  3:24
Titus 3:7
Hebrews 1:2
  6:17
  9:15
  11:7
James 2:5
1 Peter 1:3–5

CHAPTER 16: RECONCILIATION
Isaiah 52:7
  53:7
Nahum 1:15
Luke 1:79
  2:14

15:11–32
John 14:27
Acts 10:36
Romans 1:22–23
  5:1
  5:9–11
  11:12
  11:15
  15:13
2 Corinthians 5:11–21
Ephesians 2:14–17
  6:15
Philippians 4:7
Colossians 1:19–20ff
  3:15

CHAPTER 17: PEACE
Numbers 6:26
Psalm 85:8
  29:11
  119:165
Isaiah 9:6–7
  26:3
  27:5
  32:17
  48:18
  52:7
  53:7
  54:10
  55:12
  57:2
  57:19
  57:21
  60:17
  66:12
Jeremiah 6:14
  8:11

30:10
33:6
46:27
Ezekiel 37:26–28
Micah 5:5a
Nahum 1:15
Haggai 2:9
Zechariah 9:10
Matthew 5:9
  10:34
Luke 1:79
  2:14
  24:36
John 14:27
  16:33
Acts 10:36
Romans 5:1
  14:17
  15:13
Colossians 1:19–20ff
  3:15
Ephesians 2:14–17
  6:15
Philippians 4:7
1 Thessalonians 3:16
  5:23
2 Timothy 2:22
Hebrews 7:2
  12:11
James 3:13–18

CHAPTER 18: FORGIVENESS
Exodus 34:7
34:9
Numbers 14:19–20
Psalm 32:5
65:3
85:2
103:3
130:4
Isaiah 33:24
58:6
61:1
Jeremiah 31:34
33:8
36:3
50:20
Matthew 6:14–15
9:5–6
12:31–32
18:21–35
26:28
Mark 1:4
2:1–12
3:29
Luke 1:77
3:3
4:18
7:36–50
24:47
John 20:23

Acts 2:38
5:31
10:43
13:38
26:18
Romans 4:7
Ephesians 1:7
Colossians 1:13–14
Hebrews 9:22
10:18
1 John 1:9
2:12

CHAPTER 19: MARRIAGE
Psalm 19:4b–5
Song of Songs 2:4
3:11
Isaiah 49:18
54:5
61:10
62:5
Jeremiah 2:32
3:14
3:20
7:34
16:9
25:10
31:32
33:11
Ezekiel 16:32
Hosea (the entire book)
Joel 2:16

John 19:17
Romans 3:25
  5:9–10
  6:10–11
  6:13
  6:16
  6:19
  12:1
1 Corinthians 5:7
  6:20
  11:27
Ephesians 2:13
  5:2
Colossians 1:20
Hebrews 7:26–27
  9
  10:1–18
  13:12
  1 Peter 1:2
  1:19
1 John 1:7
Revelation 1:5
  5:9
  7:14
  12:11

CHAPTER 22: HALLOWING/
CLEANSING
  Cleansing
  Leviticus 15:30
    17:11
  Ruth 3:3

Psalm 51:2,
  51:7
  51:10
Proverbs 20:9
  20:30
Isaiah 1:15
  1:16
  1:18
  4:4
Jeremiah 2:22
  13:27
  33:8
Lamentations 1:18
  1:27
Ezekiel 36:25
  36:33
Zechariah 13:1
Matthew 5:8
  8:2
  23:25–26
John 13:1–17
  15:3
  17:14
Acts 10:9–23
  15:9
  22:16
Ephesians 5:25–27
Titus 2:14
Hebrews 1:3
  9:13–14
  9:22
  10:22
1 Peter 3:21

2 Peter 1:9
1 John 1:7
  1:9
Hallowing
Deuteronomy 32:51
Psalm 93:5
Isaiah 29:23
  35:8–10
  43:3
  54:5
Matthew 6:9
John 17:17
  17:19
Acts 9:13
  9:32
  26:10
Romans 1:7
  8:27
  15:25
  15:26
  15:31
  16:2
  15:15
1 Corinthians 1:2
  1:30
  6:1
  6:11
2 Corinthians 1:1
Ephesians 1:1
  1:15
  2:19
  3:8
  5:25–27

Philippians 1:1
  4:22
Colossians 1:4
  3:12
2 Thessalonians 2:13
1 Timothy 5:10
Philemon 5
Hebrews 2:11
  6:10
  9:13–14
  10:10
  13:12
1 Peter 1:2

CHAPTER 23: SALVATION
Exodus 15:2
Psalm 13:5
  27:1
  28:8–9
  37:39–40
  51:12
  51:14
  62:1–2
  62:6–7
  85:9
  98:1–3
  145:19

Isaiah 12:2
  17:10
  19:20
  25:9
  27:9
  33:6
  33:22
  35:4
  43:3
  43:11
  45:15
  45:17
  45:21
  46:13
  49:26
  51:5–6
  51:8
  52:10
  59:16
  59:20–21
  60:16
  61:10
  62:11
  63:8
Jeremiah 14:8
Joel 2:28–32
Matthew 1:21
  10:22

Mark 5:23
  5:28
  5:34
  6:56
  8:35
  10:26
  10:52
  13:13
Luke 1:47
  2:11
  7:50
  8:12
  8:36
  8:50
  17:19
  18:26
  19:9–10
John 3:17
  5:34
  10:9
Acts 2:21
  4:12
  5:31
  13:23
  15:1
  16:30–31
  28:28
Romans 1:16
  5:9
  10:9
  10:13
  11:26–27
  13:11